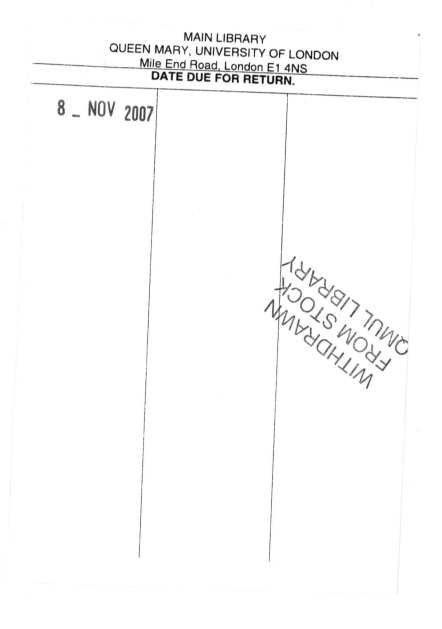

THOMAS CAMPION:
DE PULUEREA CONIURATIONE

LEEDS TEXTS AND MONOGRAPHS
New Series 10

GENERAL EDITORS
Stanley Ellis and Peter Meredith

THOMAS CAMPION:
DE PULUEREA CONIURATIONE
(On the Gunpowder Plot)

Sidney Sussex MS 59

Edited by
DAVID LINDLEY

with translation and additional notes by
ROBIN SOWERBY

LEEDS TEXTS AND MONOGRAPHS
New Series 10

Leeds Studies in English
1987

Campion, Thomas
    De puluerea coniuratione = (On the
    Gunpowder Plot): Sidney Sussex MS 59. –
    (Leeds texts and monographs. New series,
    ISSN 0075-8574; v. 10).
    I. Title II. Lindley, David III. Sowerby,
    Robin IV. University of Leeds *School of
    English* V. Series
    871'.04 PR2228.D3

ISSN 0075-8574
ISBN 0-902296-20-5

Printed in Great Britain by
the University Printing Service at the University of Leeds

for *Leeds Studies in English*

CONTENTS

ACKNOWLEDGEMENTS

In the course of preparing this edition, help has generously been offered in a variety of ways. Leeds University School of English gave grants towards the microfilming of the manuscript and covered the cost of travel to Cambridge. Mrs. Enid Nixon, Assistant Librarian of Westminster Abbey, gave helpful information on the tomb of Queen Elizabeth. Godfrey Waller, Superintendent of the Manuscript Reading Room at the Cambridge University Library, and his staff were unfailingly cheerful in their assistance. Advice on the collation of the manuscript and on the handwriting was offered by Dr. Dorothy Owen and Mr. Arthur Owen. The generous help of Dr. Vivien Law, the Archivist of Sidney Sussex College, in placing the mansucript on deposit in the Cambridge University Library, and especially in assisting with the deciphering of the pasted-down leaf of the manuscript was invaluable, and our debt to her is great. In the preparation of the copy Dr. Jon Duke of the Leeds University Computing Services devised programmes, and aided a beginner's incompetence in a number of ways.

Peter Beal, by drawing my attention to the existence of this manuscript, initiated the project. The edition is made possible by kind permission of the Master and Fellows of Sidney Sussex. To them this book is respectfully offered.

David Lindley
Robin Sowerby
Leeds, 1987

INTRODUCTION

The Manuscript

The manuscript of this, by far Campion's longest and most
ambitious Latin poem, is housed in Sidney Sussex College, Cam-
bridge. There it has lain since some time in the early seven-
teenth century, and though listed by M. R. James in his catalogue
of Sidney Sussex MSS[1] it was overlooked by Campion's editors,
until its existence was once again noted by Peter Beal in his
Index of Literary Manuscripts.[2]
   The MS itself is in an early nineteenth century binding, with
two fly-leaves and paste-down of presumably the same date. It
contains three leaves at back and front of a thinner paper than
the body of the text. On the first of these leaves, in secretary
hand, is written "Liber Collegii Domine Franciscae Sydney-Sus-
sex". The second is blank, the third is inscribed "Thomae Cam-
piani Londinatis,/D: Med:/ De puluerea coniuratione/Libri 2o".
The leaves of the manuscript, measuring 6 ins. by 7.5 ins., are
ruled to produce boxes of 4.25 by 6.5 ins. in the body of the
text, with a double margin at the outer edges. (The two pages of
epigrams do not have the double margin.) The first two leaves
contain the prefatory epigrams, with lines ruled precisely for
each epigram. The second of these leaves is glued to the first
of the three gatherings of four leaves, each of which has a
catchword on the verso of the last leaf. Two leaves complete the
text of 'Liber 1'. 'Liber 2' is made up of three gatherings of
four leaves. The verso of the final leaf is blank, but ruled with
the twenty-five lines which are standard throughout the text
itself.
   The poem is written throughout in a clear italic hand, prob-
ably by a single scribe (though the writing shows some evidence
of greater haste in the latter part of the book). Scattered
throughout the poem, however, are corrections written on slips of
paper pasted over the text. (These slips are indicated by [ ] in
the transcription.) They are written in a darker ink than the
body of the manuscript and may possibly be in a different hand.
The most significant such correction is of the first leaf of the
MS, where a whole page, containing the prefatory epigram to the
King, is pasted over an original prose dedication.
   A strong light and considerable patience make it possible to

decipher almost all of the obscured dedication to James (tran-
scribed in the Notes, p. 97),   but it is impossible to discern
what lies underneath the smaller correction slips, save that some
at least of the corrections are substantive revisions, not merely
righting errors cf transcription.   (A small number of minor cor-
rections are made in the MS by writing over erasures.)
     The one surviving signature in Campion's hand (reproduced as
the frontispiece of Vivian's edition of his works) is insuffi-
cient evidence to support any conjecture that the corrections may
actually have been written by him, though the "Tho. Campion" at
the bottom of the pasted-over dedication is clearly not in his
hand. But the manuscript was evidently produced under his close
supervision, and was carefully revised before being presented.
(The incidence of correction slips is higher in the first part of
the poem, though emendations are to be found throughout, up to
the final page of the mansucript.)
     The only problem that the manuscript poses for the transcriber
concerns the punctuation. Commas in particular are carelessly
placed, sometimes very faint and below the line of text. Some
marks may be no more than a scribal resting of the pen before
continuing with the next line. There are one or two places where
emendation has seemed to be necessary,   and some others where no
firm decision can be made about the punctuation.
     Evidence for the dating of the manuscript is entirely internal
to the work.   In it Campion alludes to the death of Prince Henry
(I. 630) and of John Harington, when he accompanied Princess
Elizabeth and her husband abroad (II. 120).   The recording of
these events, which took place in 1612 and 1613 respectively,
provides the earliest date at which the poem in its present form
could have been written.   The fifth epigram addresses John Donne
as "Doctor". He only achieved this title in 1615,[3] and so the
manuscript must have been prepared in its final form after that
date. This epigram, however, is written in the darker ink of the
alterations and emendations, and therefore does not exclude the
possibility of earlier compostion for the bulk of the work.   It
is possible that the reference to Princess Elizabeth as "soon to
be the mother of sons" (II. 113) represents knowledge of the
birth of her second son in 1617 - but the phrase could equally
well be a fairly conventional hope for the future and cannot be
regarded as sure evidence for dating purposes.
     There is even less concrete evidence for the latest date at
which the manuscript could have been prepared, and here, perhaps,
there is a mystery to be considered. Campion issued a second
edition of his Latin works in 1619, and it must be asked why he
did not include this poem in that publication.   It is

theoretically possible that the work was completed too late for
inclusion, which would place it very precisely in 1619/20, before
Campion's death on 1 March, 1620.   In view of the length of the
poem, however, and the scrupulousness of the revision of the MS,
this would seem inherently improbable.

There is, however, another possibility. Leicester Bradner sug-
gested that "at some time between 1595 and 1619 Campion had
secretly joined the Roman church".[4] His evidence is chiefly
that "the only two passages offensive to Catholics in the 1595
volume, Ad Thamesin (on the defeat of the Armada) and Elegia I,
are among the poems omitted in revision". If his hypothesis were
true, then it might just be possible that a conversion to Catho-
licism led Campion to suppress this later anti-Catholic poem
(which, interestingly enough, praises Elizabeth's restoration of
the purity of the British church in terms very similar to those
of his earlier Armada poem).

It seems, however, much more likely that the suggestion of
Campion's conversion is itself mistaken. No such hypothesis is
really needed to explain the omission of Ad Thamesin from the
later publication. It is addressed to the then living Queen
Elizabeth and would have needed substantial revision to make its
later publication appropriate. Moreoever, Campion may well have
come to recognise - not least through the experience of writing
the present work - that it is in many ways clumsy in its effort
to combine mythology and history. As Davis comments, it is a
"curious piece", so intent on "descriptive pieces" that Campion
"left a scant eighteen lines for the defeat itself, and then
broke that off for an apostrophe to Elizabeth".[5] It is surely
an artistic, rather than a religious motive which is sufficient
to explain the omission of this poem from the later collection.
Far from supporting Bradner's thesis, this work on the Gunpowder
Plot would seem to lay the ghost of Campion's Catholicism once
and for all. For while it was possible for a crypto-Catholic
such as the Earl of Northampton to figure prominently in the
trial of the conspirators, and to seek to define his position by
writing up a lengthy attack on the Jesuits for inclusion in the
official narrative of the conspiracy, A True and Perfect Rela-
tion, (1606), it is noticeable that he there confines his discus-
sion to the Jesuit doctrines of the deposition of Kings and of
equivocation, and steers carefully clear of the full-blooded con-
demnation of the Church of Rome that we find throughout Campion's
poem.[6] While many Catholics tried to distance themselves from
the plotters, no crypto-Catholic could possibly have spoken in
praise of Luther (Epigram 1; I. 89), or made the distinction
between "two religions" (I. 103ff.), or praised Elizabeth's

removal of "Latin adulteration" from the services of the church
(I. 456ff).[7] But if we may lay to rest the myth of Campion's
Catholicism, it is perhaps necessary to provide some other expla-
nation for the late date of the poem, and its absence from the
1619 Tho. Campiani Epigrammatum Libri II. There is no very obvi-
ous reason for its omission. Perhaps it was simply too long for
the later book, devoted principally to epigrams. Perhaps its
presentation to the King was too recent for it to appear in a
volume dedicated to Prince Charles. Perhaps it was simply the
case that, having presented his manuscript to the King, Campion
did not himself have another copy to provide for the printer. Or
it may be that its complimentary reference to Thomas Howard, Earl
of Suffolk, (II. 61), would have been embarrassing after his dis-
grace. Indeed this praise of the Lord Chamberlain may itself
indicate a date of composition before his fall in 1618. Compari-
son of the original prose dedication with the revised verse
inscription suggests that Campion originally intended to present
the work to the King on an anniversary of the Plot. For some rea-
son this wish must have been frustrated, and Campion had to pro-
vide a new dedication, taking the opportunity to revise details
in the poem (and perhaps to seek patronage from John Donne by
adding the complimentary fifth epigram).

The date of composition then would seem to be 1613-1620, to
give the widest possible span - or, more likely, 1615-1618. It
is, of course, entirely possible that the poem existed in an ear-
lier state and was revised for later presentation (as with other
of Campion's Latin poems).

The next question is why Campion should choose to write a poem
on the topic of the Gunpowder Plot at this point in his career.
The commemoration of the events of November 5th was firmly insti-
tuted in the calendar; special prayers were provided for use in
churches, sermons on the subject were preached and published reg-
ularly and, indeed, poets were writing on the subject for many
years to come.[8] But while there need be no special occasion for
Campion's contribution to the literature of the Plot it is possi-
ble that there was a more immediately personal reason for his
turning to the subject at this period of his life. The revela-
tion in 1615 of the murder of Thomas Overbury in the Tower had
very unfortunate implications for Campion. He had, in 1613,
written The Somerset Masque to celebrate the marriage of Frances
Howard and Robert Carr who were found guilty of the murder. His
chief patron, Sir Thomas Monson, was imprisoned because of his
involvement with the substitution of Gervase Helwes for Sir Wil-
liam Wade as Lieutenant of the Tower. Campion himself was exam-
ined for his part in handing over monies in connection with this

transaction.[9] It makes sense, then, to see the poem as an attempt to restore Campion's fading fortunes. The panegyric drift of the poem as a whole would be calculated to appeal to the King (though see below for further discussion of its political stance); its firmly anti-Catholic posture frees Campion of any charge of crypto-Catholicism, and the compliment to Thomas Howard, who had endeavoured to keep as much distance as possible between himself and his daughter throughout the disclosures of dirty deeds done in secret, strives to maintain his contact with his major court patron.

It must be doubted, however, whether the poem achieved such an aim. Campion received no further major court commission after The Somerset Masque. Monson languished in prison until 1617, though he had never been found guilty of any crime. His fortunes suffered, and it would seem from Campion's will that his protégé fared little better. Campion bequeathed "all that he had" to his friend Philip Rosseter "and wished that his estate had bin farre more".[10]

How or when the manuscript made its way to Sidney Sussex cannot be ascertained. It is possible that the work initially was handed over to James Montagu, the Master of Sidney Sussex College until 1608, who was entrusted by James with the handling of propaganda on the Gunpowder Plot, and was deeply involved with the subsequent debates on the Oath of Allegiance. The Montagu family had a continuing association with Sidney Sussex, and one might conjecture that it was through them that it was donated to the college. The absence of any record of its acquisition after 1619 perhaps suggests that it came to the college earlier. The secretary hand of the college inscription certainly suggests an early seventeenth-century date for its acquisition. There is, as far as I have been able to discover, no other copy of the poem in existence.

The Poem and History

Campion's poem is an epical panegyric, but for all its neo-Classical apparatus, especially its setting in a frame of diabolic intervention, it yet has a firm narrative base in the received story of the Gunpowder Plot. In this respect it is much more fully historical than his earlier account of the victory over the Armada in Ad Thamesin. But the work contributes nothing new to our knowledge of the actual history of the Gunpowder Plot. Its account is firmly based on two primary sources, A

True and Perfect Relation (1606), and A Discourse of the maner of
the discouery of this late Intended Treason (1606), (henceforward
referred to as Relation and Discourse), which together consti-
tuted the officially sanctioned history of the Plot.[11] Campion
may have consulted other narratives, such as that in the continu-
ation of Stow's Annals (1614), or Speed's History of Great Brit-
aine (1611). He may have derived suggestions from Valesius's In
Serenissimi Regis Iacobi (1606), and from A. P.'s translation of
Herryng's Pietas Pontifica (1610) (see notes to I. 30 and I.
680). He may even have had some first-hand memory of the events
(though there is little sign of such detail in the poem, and Cam-
pion, who took his medical degree at Caen in February 1605, may
still have been out of the country at the time of the Plot
itself).
    There has been a long-running controversy over the accuracy of
these official narratives of the events of the plot, at least
since Father Gerard's work What Was the Gunpowder Plot? (London,
1897). He suggested that the whole thing was engineered by Rob-
ert Cecil to discredit the Catholics, and that the received his-
tory is a tissue of contradictory fabrication. Many subsequent
Catholic historians, while not necessarily subscribing to this
extreme view, have more credibly sought at least to minimise the
involvement of the Jesuits, Garnet, Gerard and Tesimond. While
it is understandable, as indeed Gardiner recognised in his reply
to Gerrard, What Gunpowder Plot Was (London, 1897), pp.2-3, that
Catholic historians should urgently wish to challenge the story
which for so long was used as sufficient excuse to vilify and
oppress their co-religionists, it is difficult not to concur with
the words of Joel Hurstfield:

        the question of the authenticity of Gunpowder Plot is
        no longer a rewarding subject for historical research.
        Nothing of major significance has emerged since Gardi-
        ner examined the Plot in 1897. Trying to prove that it
        was a fabrication has become a game, like dating Shake-
        speare's sonnets: a pleasant way to pass a wet after-
        noon but hardly a challenging occupation for adult men
        and women.[12]

Campion's poem certainly offers no reason to re-open this debate.
But even if the poem offers no historical revelations, it is
still of considerable interest to observe the ways in which Cam-
pion converts his source material into a poem.
    Compression is an obvious narrative necessity. The events as
presented in the course of the accounts of the discovery of the

plot and the trial of the conspirators are disjointed, and Campion secures a smooth story by sensible editing. His account of the meeting of the conspirators after the idea of the plot has been implanted in Catesby's mind, for example (I. 176ff.), fuses the preliminary meeting of Winter, Wright and Catesby in February 1604 with their later meeting after Winter's abortive errand to seek the support of the Constable of Castile and his return in the company of Fawkes. In rather similar fashion Campion constructs a meeting of the Jesuits after the discovery of the Plot out of two distinct episodes, omitting altogether the despatch of Tesimond to convey the news to Oldcorne (Hall). Some small additions are made to the reported speeches with the aim of improving narrative coherence. Most notably, perhaps, we find the addition to Winter's early speech of the fear that "a fair portion of our persuasion will fall" (I. 217), which solidifies the importance of Catesby's reassurance by Garnet of the morality of sacrificing a few for the greater cause (I. 359ff.). To make the work a more artful history, however, Campion accepts the traditional licence to supplement and invent speeches for his characters, most markedly in the conversations of the Jesuits and of the conspirators towards the end of the poem. These speeches serve to flesh out the characters of the main protagonists, and Campion shows himself ready to clarify these figures as types, emphasising, for example, Winter's fearfulness and Percy's fieriness by some judicious reallocation of words and sentiments attributed variously to the conspirators in the sources. Campion concentrates on those characters who figure most prominently in the official sources, particularly in the confessions of Fawkes and Winter in Discourse, and the account of Garnet's trial in Relation. The other conspirators remain shadowy figures - the timetable of their recruitment is left vague, and their various responsibilities are not clarified. But narratively there is much benefit from concentration upon the main figures of "this combustible combination",[13] permitting as it does a strong forward sweep of the main story, with space for the kind of digression and amplification which directs the thematic focus of the work.

Campion's adaptation of his sources is not simply a matter of narrative convenience. Choices are made with the aim of ensuring a particular focus upon the events of the Plot. Most markedly is this the case in the treatment of the receiving of Monteagle's letter and its transmission to the King. The historical facts are unmistakeable - and Campion could not have been unaware of them, as they are to be found in Discourse, or in Howes's continuation of Stow's Annals (1614). Monteagle received his warning letter ten days before the Parliament was due and took it

immediately to Cecil. Cecil and Suffolk considered the letter
and, as Cecil's letter to Cornwallis makes quite clear, both of
them had a pretty shrewd suspicion of what the nature of the
threat might be:

> we both conceaved, that it could not be more proper
> than the time of Parliament, nor by any other way like
> to be attempted than with Powder, whilst the King was
> sitting in that Assembly.[14]

The King, as so often, was away at Royston hunting - hence Cam-
pion's tactful remark about Cecil, "to whom has been handed over
the care of the realm" (I. 650-1). The members of the Council
decided not to inform him until "some three or four Daies before
the Sessions". In the event it was not until 3 November that the
letter was shown to him and, though much was to be made of his
perspicuity in resolving the riddle, Salisbury in his letter
merely remarks upon the King's sensible agreement that chances
should not be taken. The Earl of Suffolk as Lord Chamberlain was
instructed to make a preliminary search (an incident Campion
omits). Though he uncovered nothing, Suffolk's anxiety was
aroused by learning that the cellar was leased to Percy. His
report led to the ordering of a further search by Knyvett at
about eleven at night with the consequent discovery of the whole
enterprise.
  Campion's account, in telescoping time, places the King firmly
in the centre of the action, as James himself, judging by his
self-congratulatory speech to Parliament, certainly wished. Cam-
pion's deviousness with the time-scale of events is deliberate,
and he was not alone in making this effort to please the King.
Coke at the trial of the conspirators was similarly evasive, and
John Speed in his account gets over the uncomfortable gap in the
time-sequence by having the King perceive the truth earlier, but
order his counsellors to wait before doing anything.[15] Campion,
like other writers, was quite unashamed in bending the known
sequence of events in order to compliment the King upon his
prophetic perspicacity, thereby confirming his intention, sig-
nalled in both versions of the opening dedication, to write a
panegyric poem.
  Most significant of all for the design of Campion's poem, how-
ever, is the way he follows the official version of the history
of the Plot in asserting the role of the Jesuits as the arch con-
spirators. While modern historians, even those of Protestant
leanings, concur in regarding the evidence produced against them
as less than fully convincing, there is no mistaking the

universal desire of contemporaries to implicate them as fully as
possible in the devising of the whole scheme. At the indictment
of the conspirators they are placed at the forefront, as those
who did "maliciously, falsly, and traiterously mooue and per-
swade" the others to rebellion "for the aduancing and enlargement
of the pretended Authority and Iurisdiction of the Bishop of
Rome, and for the restoring of the superstitious romish Religion
within the Realme of England".[16] Later Coke asserted bluntly:
"the principall offenders are the seducing Iesuits, men that vse
the reuerence of Religion, yea euen the most Sacred and blessed
name of IESVS as a mantle to couer their impietie, blasphemie,
treason and Rebellion".[17]

It is important to ask why it should have been so necessary to
implicate the Jesuits in the Gunpowder Plot.   Derek Hirst
observes: "Perhaps the most obvious feature of political analysis
in the period is the prevalence of what another age has come to
know as conspiracy theory".[18] Carol Z. Weiner, analysing this
phenomenon, suggests that when Englishmen of the period looked at
the Roman Church "they rarely saw a collection of disparate indi-
viduals, each with his own aims and methods. What they saw was a
highly organized and united front".[19] It is straightforward
enough to see the desperate attempts to implicate the Jesuits as
a product of these attitudes and anxieties. The prayers in the
liturgy instituted to commemorate the safe deliverance of the
country from the Plot are clear enough confirmation of such
attitudes, as they appeal to God:

> Be thou still our mighty Protector, and scatter our
> cruel enemies, which delight in blood: infatuate their
> counsels, and roote out that Babylonish and Anti-Chris-
> tian sect, which say of Jerusalem, Downe with it, downe
> with it, euen to the ground. And to that ende
> strengthen the handes of our gracious King, the Nobles
> and Magistrates of the Land with iudgement and iustice
> to cut off these workers of iniquitie (whose Religion
> is Rebellion, whose faith is faction, whose practise is
> murthering of soules and bodies) and to root them out
> of the confines and limits of this kingdom.

But while Campion's poem does indeed attack the false religion of
Rome, notably in the hellish picture of the one-eyed goddess and
the gaudy palace (I. 109-121), it is nonetheless significant,
both for his poem and indeed for much other contemporary writing
on the Plot that the Jesuits in particular should be singled out.
James himself in his speech to Parliament on 9 November observed:

> I would be sorrie that any being innocent of this prac-
> tise, either domesticall or forraine, should receiue
> blame or harme for the same. For although it cannot be
> denied, That it was the onely blinde superstition of
> their errors in Religion, that led them to this desper-
> ate deuice; yet doth it not follow, That all professing
> that Romish religion were guiltie of the same.[20]

It must be said that it is this remarkably tolerant understanding
which Campion himself chooses to omit as he toughens up James's
speech in his own account of it (II. 190-221), yet the strategic
importance of blaming the Jesuits lies in its necessary attempt
to distinguish a particularly dangerous faction in the Roman
church from those Catholics with whom, willy-nilly, English soci-
ety had to cope. That this is to some degree the case can be seen
from the way in which the Oath of Allegiance, devised as a direct
result of the fears generated by the Plot, was presented by the
King and his apologists as intended to distinguish loyal Catho-
lics from those dangerously liable to disaffection.[21] No doubt
this is to simplify dangerously, but yet the plea of one Catholic
writer suggests that many of his co-religionists saw some hope in
distancing themselves from the outrage. He condemned the Plot,
saying it was:

> so heinous impiety, that nothing which is holy can make
> it legitimate; no practice of Religion can be alleged
> to excuse it . . . Protestants exclaime against it, and
> your dutiful, Religious and learned Catholikes,
> Priests, and others, which haue endured most for their
> profession, hold it in greater horror, and make it a
> subiect of their grieuous sorrow, that any of their
> profession should attempt so barbarous and vnnaturall
> cruelty, or practise any disobedience at all to your
> Highnesse.[22]

The Jesuits, then, might in some ways be seen as merely typical
of the threat of the Roman enemy; but it was equally important in
pragmatic political terms to attempt to place the blame for the
Plot on a group who could be detached from 'ordinary' Catholics.
(In making such a distinction the Government were doing no more
than building upon the internal divisions within the Catholic
Mission between the secular priests and the Jesuits which had
surfaced at the time of the Apellant controversy, and were to
continue through the next decades.)
    The hysterical reaction which the Order generated can be

typified by the words of Thomas James in The Iesuits Downfall (1612):

> In all sacrilegious and temporizing platformes, Atheall
> plots of perdition, Matchiavellian or rather Mahumetan-
> like faction, Heathenish, tyrannical, Sathanicall and
> Turkish gouernment, none goeth beyond the Iesuits at
> this day; and they are able to set Aretin, Lucian,
> Matchiavel, yea and Don Lucifer in a sort to schoole,
> as impossible for him by all the Art he hath, to besot
> men as they do (p. 20).

There are perhaps three main reasons for the particular loathing that the Jesuits generated. The first was recognised by the Jesuit writer of the Annual Letter of 1614:

> We are called the Pope's janissaries; the favourite
> brood of antichrist; the sworn slaves of the
> Pope . . . They say that hell has sent us forth fully
> equipped with learning and other gifts, both natural
> and acquired, in order to prop up those of the Papacy,
> now tottering to its fall.[23]

It is precisely this threat that Donne articulated:

> The Supernumerary Vowe of the Iesuites, by which they
> doe especially oblige themselues to the Popes will,
> doth in the nature, and Essence, and scope thereof,
> make them enemies to the dignitie of all Princes,
> because their Soueraigntie cannot consist, with that
> temporall Supremacie which the Iesuites must maintaine,
> by the obligation of that vow, by which they are bound,
> with expense of their life, to penetrate any Kingdome,
> and instill Sedition into their Disciples and follow-
> ers.[24]

It is this 'special relationship' with the Papal Antichrist which contributes to the particular menace of the Jesuits, and their usefulness as epitomes of the internationalist threat the Papacy seemed to offer to the ever-strengthening nationalism of Tudor and Stuart society. The author of A Discouerie of the Most Secret and Subtile Practises of the IESUITES (1610) asserted, for example, that they were plotting to estrange the princes of the Empire and "to plant in theyre place the tiranny of Spaine and the Popes primacy in Germany" (Sig. B1v).

But Donne's comment suggests also the second major reason for
the singling out of the Jesuits - their threat to the temporal
sovereignty of Kings.   It would be inappropriate here to trace
the history of Jesuit involvement with debates about the nature
of Kingship and the right of subjects to depose an 'heretical'
monarch.   The controversy had begun in the aftermath of the
excommunication of Queen Elizabeth, and formed a major part of
the international debate which followed upon James's publication
of his Apology for the Oath of Allegiance.[25]   It is sufficient
to remark that the Jesuit attitude to kingship,   expressed for
example in Doleman's Conferences (1595), is one of the key
sources of their unattractiveness to James and his divine right
aspirations. For, as Thomas H. Clancy observes at the end of his
detailed study of the subject: "throughout the seventeenth cen-
tury the doctrine of popular sovreignty was identified by the
defenders of royal power as 'the Jesuit poison'".[26] A symptom
of its significance to the mental world of those who sought to
implicate the Jesuits in the Plot is the learned display made by
Northampton (with the help of Robert Cotton) in his lengthy con-
tribution to Relation.
    The particular closeness of the Jesuits to the Pope and their
espousal of the right to depose 'heretical' monarchs form sig-
nificant strands in Campion's poem.   They are alluded to clearly
in the third Epigram, in the speech of the hooded devil (I.
84ff.), the lament for decayed times (I. 129ff.) and in the
speech of the ghostly Ignatius (II. 357ff.), for example. But it
is the third of the common charges brought against the Jesuits -
their doctrine of equivocation - which is perhaps most signifi-
cant for the poem as a whole.
    Garnet's treatise on equivocation was found amongst Tresham's
papers (though his authorship was apparently not recognised) and
was insistently alluded to during the course of his trial.   Put
simply, the doctrine allows for a Catholic being interrogated
either to use words capable of double meaning, or else to speak
out loud only part of what was in his mind, reserving the comple-
tion of the idea in his head. This 'mental reservation' would,
for example, allow Garnet to answer 'No' to the question: 'Did
you know of the Gunpowder Plot?', reserving in his mind the con-
tinuation 'not under conditions which might allow me to disclose
my knowledge' (since he learnt of the Plot under the seal of the
confessional).[27] It is not at all difficult to see why this
doctrine should seem so dangerous to men in authority.   Robert
Cecil called it: "that most strange and grosse doctrine of Equi-
uocation, which is so highly extolled in the Church of Rome,
though it teare in sunder all the bondes of humane

conuersation".[28] A characteristic invective against the prac-
tice is found in The Iesuits Downfall (1612):

> No one thing breedeth greater danger and hatred to all
> Catholikes in England, than the Iesuits abuse of Equi-
> vocating, making it indeed nothing else but an art of
> lying, cogging, foisting and forging, and that without
> al respect of matter, time, place, person . . . or
> other circumstance (pp. 16-17).

Northampton and Coke returned repeatedly to the issue in the
trial of Garnet, seeking to undermine any trust in his assertions
of innocence. While Garnet himself, and Robert Parsons in his
lengthy defence of the practice in A Treatise Tending to Mitiga-
tion (1607), with its subtle consideration of rhetoric and signi-
fication, could both insist that equivocation was not lying, the
distinction was one which Garnet's judges were not prepared to
make. To them it was but explicit proof of the dangerous duplic-
ity of the Jesuits, and was taken as "the high point" on which
Garnet "must satisfy the King, that he may know what to trust
unto".[29] And, as Malloch observes:

> If equivocation could appear to Catholics a providen-
> tial solution to their dilemma of conscience, it could
> equally appear to Protestants a providential means of
> destroying the credibility of Catholics. The story of
> how indignation against the doctrine was used to dis-
> credit Jesuits in particular and Catholics in general
> is a story that centres about Henry Garnet himself: his
> unhappy experiments in the Tower with the very doctrine
> he had defended in his treatise, his consequent help-
> lessness before accusation, and the role he was des-
> tined to play as the prototype of the equivocating Jes-
> uit.[30]

Campion makes repeated reference to the practice of equivocation
and, as will be seen later, it is this duplicity of the Jesuits
which is perhaps most significant for his thematic purposes. But
at this stage it is sufficient to observe that throughout his
history of the Plot he follows and even strengthens the official
verdict on the Jesuits' complicity. Gerard is implicated by his
administration of the sacrament to the original band of conspira-
tors; Garnet's guilty knowledge of the plot direct from Catesby
is blandly asserted; the instrumental role of Tesimond in raising
rumours of Catholic persecution is stressed in the final

denouement of the conspiracy.

It is, therefore, surprising but not inexplicable that Campion should simply avoid the crucial question upon which the demonstration of Garnet's guilt turned. For at his trial Garnet agreed that he knew of the Plot, having received information about it under the seal of confession from Tesimond, who had himself learnt of it from Bates's confession to him. The trial judges were determined to prove that Garnet could and should have used this information to alert the authorities, or at least to forbid the action itself. Since the debate turned upon the secrecy of the confessional it was a ticklish one, even for Protestants, and Campion in his poem has little concern with such problematic issues. For though his work is, as we have seen, closely based on the historical narratives, it is concerned ultimately with something more than the minutiae of circumstantial detail. Its greatest interest for the modern reader, indeed, lies precisely in the ways in which it exemplifies and encodes the attitudes that the historical event allowed to be articulated.

Structure and Implication

After his Christianised epic invocation Campion plunges straight into his major 'fiction' in the poem, the Satanic council which instigates the idea of the Plot. It is not difficult to see why he chose this device. Apart from classical and Renaissance epic precedents for underworld journeys and the explication of human events by mythic apparatus, the facts of the Plot itself (whether or not the 'cellar' was actually underground)[31] are sufficient to explain the appropriateness of the fiction. In one way or another most writers built upon it. John Speed, for example, characterised it in his History as:

> A stratagem inuented by him that blowes the bellowes of
> destruction, fashioned in the forge of the bottomlesse
> pitte, put in practise in a vault of darknesse, and
> forwarded by him that is the father of darkenesse.
>   (p.889)

Other authors developed their story of the Plot in similar ways. Michael Valesius's In Serenissimi Regis Iacobi (1606), Francis Herryng's Pietas Pontifica (1606),[32] William Gager's Pyramis Quinto Novembris 1605[33] and Pineas Fletcher's Locustae (of which the earliest MS dates from about 1611)[34] all include some

sort of hellish debate and instigation of the Plot.   Add to that
the familiar depiction of the Jesuits as children of Satan, their
presentation in a hellish council in Donne's Ignatius his Con-
clave (to which Campion refers explicitly in Epigram 5)   and the
growing fashion for satirical works containing journeys to the
underworld,[35] and it is obvious that there was no scarcity of
suggestion for Campion's decision so to initiate his narrative.
In point of fact, he needed to look no further than his own Ad
Thamesin, which ascribed the setting out of the Armada to a plot
hatched in the underworld.
    But, of course, the choice of this particular device speaks
more than a decision about narrative structure, more than a mere
desire to inflate the significance of the events it relates by
hyperbole. At one level it reflects a deep-rooted belief that
human history is not explicable solely in human terms.   In the
sixteenth century, as for centuries before, events were explained
primarily as the working out of God's design.   The discovery of
the Plot was therefore easily to be seen as a clear sign of God's
protection of his new-chosen Israel,   Britain and its Protestant
church.   It is precisely in this way that Campion himself pre-
sented the Plot in the second stanza of his lyric "Bravely
deckt":

                Britaines, frolicke at your bourd,
                But first sing praises to the Lord
                     In your Congregations.
                Hee preserv'd your state alone,
                His loving grace hath made you one
                     Of his chosen Nations.[36]

    At the same time, however, the removal of the events of the
Plot on to this cosmic stage has another, quite distinct function
and effect, at least to the eyes of the modern commentator.   In
its refusal to contemplate particular causes for the events of
1605 it represents the ideology of those in authority in the
early Stuart court in interesting ways.   Carol Weiner is puzzled
by the fact that Stuart commentators were so so ready to blame
the Plot on a global Catholic conspiracy:

        Reputable historians, even those of Protestant sympa-
        thies, have seen in Gunpowder Treason the natural fruit
        of Catholic despair. Given the conditions of Catholic
        life in England at this time, and considering the fact
        that the minority's hopes for some improvement had been
        raised, only to be thwarted in the first years of the

new King's reign, the modern historian must only wonder
that more such desperate plans did not evolve. The
recognition of these natural causes of the Plot might
have given the English some comfort or sense of control
over their situation. To see the Pope's hand in the
Treason, to perceive it as a work of giant and sinister
proportions, did nothing to help them.[37]

All those who spoke or wrote about the Plot insisted, again
and again, that there was no reason for the actions of the con-
spirators. James himself, in Triplici Nodo, spoke of the treason
as "plotted without cause, infinite in crueltie, and singular
from all examples".[38] Tirelessly did other writers assert that
James's conduct towards the Catholics was of unexampled mildness,
far exceeding the practice of his predecessor Queen Elizabeth. To
them the Catholic sense of grievance was simply incomprehensible.
Campion goes some small way to support this view by his insis-
tence on the social class of the conspirators. We are told early
on that they were "notables" (I.   155), reminded that digging a
mine was an unlikely occupation for men of their position (I.
416ff.), and presented with the troubled figure of Digby "whom
his own lot made fortunate" (II. 99). How, he seems to be saying,
could men of such position and fortune, be brought into a plot of
this kind except by diabolic seduction?   It was the Catholic
apologists, Parsons pre-eminent amongst them, for whom the asser-
tion of 'realistic' causes of the Plot was essential.   They
blamed James for falsely raising hopes of toleration amongst the
Catholics; they depicted the sufferings, spiritual and financial,
which recusants endured.   For those in authority to admit that
James had deceived the Catholics, or that his policy was unjust
and occasioned reasonable anger, let alone to take cognisance of
that anti-Scottish feeling which Jenny Wormald has convincingly
suggested as a significant spur to the action,[39] would be to
compromise the King and to admit a notion of history and causal-
ity which represented a far more fundamental threat to the ideol-
ogy of the court than Weiner seems prepared to allow. In a para-
doxical fashion, then, it was more not less comforting to cast
the Plot as a diabolic attempt, rather than a rational, if mis-
guided, response to the actuality of religious policy. Catesby
as the Devil's tool was less dangerous than Catesby the disgrun-
tled individual - his crime could be accommodated within offi-
cialdom's view of itself with much greater ease.
    To say this is not simply to accuse the judges, Coke in par-
ticular, of falsifying evidence (though they were quite prepared
to do so).   The rhetoric of the trial grows out of an urgent

ideological necessity to suppress a rational, causal explanation
of the Plot, deriving from a mixture of attitudes and presupposi-
tions about the Monarchy, about the religious contest of which
the Plot could be taken as a symptom, and about the nature of
historical explanation itself. Campion's poem, in choosing to
emphasise by its Satanic framework the working of providence at
the expense of 'realistic' analysis of cause and effect, is not
essentially at variance with the underlying attitudes of the
trial judges. It simply clarifies their presuppositions, as it
omits, for example, any question of economic motivation on the
part of the conspirators, or detail about the early growth of the
Plot and its continuation from the so-called Spanish Treason.
Instead we find the Plot described at the beginning of the poem
as the most marvellous example of God's intervention in human
affairs. This view of events was reduplicated endlessly. Robert
Cecil, for example, wrote:

> Let vs make it appeare vnto the world, by the differ-
> ence of our constant measure of thankefullnesse, that
> we esteeme not this an ordinary acte of Gods Provi-
> dence, nor a thing to be imputed to any fault or fayl-
> ing in their plots or proiects, but a miraculous effect
> of the transcendent power, farre beyond the course and
> compasse of all his ordinary proceedings. [40]

Not only are the causes of the plot to be masked, but even the
wit of those who caused it to be discovered is played down in the
mystification and mythification of the event.

It is in this context that the remarkable digression of the
speech of Pia Relligio at the tomb of Queen Elizabeth acquires
its force. Her victories over the Roman enemy are celebrated,
and, we are told: "the One God protected her with his love, and
saved her from all perils" (I. 461). The speech picks up issues
raised elswhere in the poem. Characteristic is the way in which
her determined opposition to the Jesuits is favourably contrasted
with the temporising of Henri IV of France, who took down the
Pyramid, sign of his banishment of the Jesuits, and was subse-
quently assassinated by them (I. 327 ff.). (Campion, indeed,
compresses time to make the point more forceful, since it was not
"as soon as" the momument was taken down that Henry perished, but
some six years later.) The poem insists upon the way in which
James inherited from her, took over, as it were, the causes that
she had furthered. The point is affirmed by its placement at the
heart of Satan's lament at the beginning of the poem, where he
complains that the new King is just as much an enemy as his

predecessor. It is picked up again with renewed insistence in
this speech (I. 485 ff.). This urging of the continuity between
Elizabeth and James and the contrast made with France is all part
of the same effort to characterise the salvation from the Plot as
instance of God's special care of his chosen nation. The elabo-
rate apostrophe of Pia Relligio allows this assertion its full
voice.[41]

    The epical machinery, of course, is a vital element in moving
the Plot onto a plane removed from realistic patterns of cause
and effect. Specifically, each stage of the action is initiated
by the other world. A messenger from the devil suggests the idea
of the Plot itself to Catesby; a rather peculiar flying devil
wings Winter to Belgium (I. 291ff.) and "companionable spirits"
aid the digging of the mine (I. 423). Ignatius rises from hell
to suggest the sowing of seditious rumour in the last stages of
the conspiracy (II. 352ff.). On the other side, it is a winged
visitor from heaven who consoles Pia Relligio and then delivers
the note to Monteagle (no suggestion here of treachery amongst
the conspirators). It is through the "unconscious foresight" of
Divine prompting that the calling of Parliament is postponed, and
through the intervention of the "youth from heaven" that Greville
is inspired to action in the last stages of the Plot (II.
459ff.).

    This dematerialisation of the causes of the Plot is a vital
symptom of the underlying ideology of Campion's poem, and it
enables the most significant structural feature of the work, as
it sets up the struggle between Satan and God as the 'real' story
of the Plot. The whole design of the work is built upon pat-
terned contrasts. Protestantism and Catholicism are contrasted
in the familiar opposition of simplicity and gaudiness. There are
two lakes of tears, one for the penitent, one for the tears of
rage. The opposition of hellish and heavenly visitants has
already been remarked. On a larger scale Satan's abuse of God
(I. 50ff.) is answered by James's dutiful prayer (II. 190ff.), as
the hellish conclave of the opening is answered by the Parliament
of the beginning of Book Two. The apostrophe to 'Impia Relligio'
(I. 128ff.) is contrasted with the long speech of 'Pia Relligio'
over the tomb of Queen Elizabeth (I. 470ff.). At the most obvi-
ous level such contrasts give a strength and solidity to the
design of the poem.

    There is, however, much greater significance to this effort of
polarisation. While superficially Campion seems simply to be
lining up the 'goodies' and 'baddies' in unmistakeable fashion,
the very effort to do so is a mark of the way the events of 1605
raised difficult and uncomfortable problems of moral distinction.

The fundamental question is raised in Egerton's speech, when he
observes ironically: "If you ask from whence this crime spreads,
religion is the culprit that breeds crime, piety is the same and
truly thirsts for plunder" (II. 147-50). The Catholic conspira-
tors believe that what they do is for God, and for their relig-
ion. So, when Baynham is despatched to Rome, he carries "news of
this holy work that is full of glory and heaven-blessed merit"
(I. 580); and when Fawkes is discovered he is utterly unrepen-
tant, confessing the deed, and taking pride in it as "something
justified and serving heaven" (II. 44). It is precisely the con-
spirators' belief in divine sanction of their actions which made
the Plot so threatening, and necessitated a strident insistence
on their error. Few writers of the period could afford to look
squarely at the problems, as Donne did in his "Satire 3". He
could assert: "To adore, or scorn an image, or protest/ May all
be bad" (ll. 75-6), and decry a simple appeal to authority,
observing:

> Fool and wretch, wilt thou let thy soul be tied
> To man's laws, by which she shall not be tried
> At the last day? Or will it then boot thee
> To say a Philip or a Gregory,
> A Harry, or a Martin taught thee this?
> Is not this excuse for mere contraries,
> Equally strong; cannot both sides say so? (93-99)[42]

But if writers on the Plot could not afford to allow this kind of
doubt to appear explicitly in their work, it is yet the pressure
of this kind of anxiety which fuels the Protestant determination
to insist that God is on their side. Campion's poem derives in no
small measure from the need to make it clear that in this case
"both sides" cannot claim equal authority for their beliefs, and
in its very insistence figures the suppression of disturbing
questions.
    Many writers on on the Plot express their horror at its abuse
of religion. The threat this offers is indicated by the comment
made by Francis Herryng:

> A hotchpot they, and mingle mangle make
> Of things diuine and humane, all is one,
> They make no difference[43]

It is precisely the effort to define and clarify that "mingle
mangle" which informs a great deal of Campion's poem. In his
comment on Garnet he observes "how shameful in men of religion

who confound heaven and hell" (I. 374). Many authorial comments
are similarly directed to making us aware of the conspirators'
religious delusions.   At the poem's opening Campion speaks of
"fearful deeds begun under the pretext of reverence for God" (I.
24), and later insists again and again on the "guise of pious
intention" (I. 240) under which the conspirators work. He endeav-
ours to ensure that the reader is under no such misapprehension
by continually (and conventionally) characterising the works of
Catholicism as diabolic in their disguising of the truth. Hellish
religion is characterised as "procuring a beautiful appearance
through disguise" (I. 112); the messenger decked as Hope is sent
to Catesby "painted and decked out like a high born harlot" (I.
150). The Jesuits "usurp" the name of Jesus (I. 302-3) and, like
false religion, seem "splendid at first glance", but "hideous and
revolting" when more keenly studied (I. 306-12).   It is in this
context that the Jesuit practice of equivocation is particularly
important. For, as the devil is master of disguise, so they have
taught the world to make language a tool of deception rather than
illumination. The key passage here is I. 320ff. The invention of
equivocation is not only deceptive, it is also "novel", and
stands contrasted with the "simplicity" of former times. Equivo-
cation is symptomatic of the moral perversion which Jesuits bring
about in their disciples, and the threat they pose to community.
It is, however, not just a former time of simple language which
stands opposed to the deceitful duplicity of Rome. We are also
reminded of the simplicity of true religion and the simpleness of
the ceremony restored by Elizabeth (I. 457).   But Campion is not
content to clarify the issues only by this kind of assertion.
More important to the working of the poem are the ways in which
the process of unmasking the untruthfulness of the conspirators'
religion is built into the narrative sequence.

The simplest device Campion employs is one of proleptic irony.
Satan fulminates at the beginning of the poem against those "who
know how to mollify your power by cringing prayer" (I. 68-9) —
but later his words are proved true as the heavenly visitant
assures Pia Relligio of God's protection, since "constant prayer
has proved its power" (I. 505). Winter assents to the plot, say-
ing that he will continue "even if the whole earth were to open
at my feet and the terror of the Infernal one converge upon me"
(I. 210-11), looking forward to the time when, with the visita-
tion of Ignatius, the earth will indeed open at the feet of the
Jesuits.   Catesby berates his fellow conspirators for their
delay, saying that "by phantoms we are led astray" (I. 400) —
where the reader is already aware of the phantom of hope which
has indeed led them astray.   It is as if Campion exposes the

equivocation of the Catholics by his own ironic, equivocating
voice. (For the artful punning of Campion's Latin see below,
pp. 25-7.)

But perhaps even more significant is the way in which the
whole poem is constructed to reveal to the conspirators them-
selves the delusiveness of their religious certainty. In the
early part of the poem they are clear that their action is moti-
vated by God, and though Campion is heavily ironic in describing
the way that "for shame, they look to heaven" and "call upon
Jehovah not now as a witness but as the source of their deadly
enterprise" (I. 284ff.), he yet allows us to realise that they
are, as it were, genuinely deluded. It is in the latter part of
the poem that they come to realise their illusions. After the
Plot has gone wrong Wright complains "what dark action of the
devil brought the hidden deeds to light" (II. 249-50), still mak-
ing the "mingle-mangle" of heaven and hell. Shortly, however,
Garnet is worriedly claiming that "such endeavours I believe
never sufficiently pleased God", and recognising that the protec-
tion of Elizabeth and her successor might indeed be a sign that
God is on the opposition's side (II. 320ff.). Hall makes a last
stand in rallying the troops, with his attempt to prove that
defeat does not necessarily indicate that God is not with them
(II. 333ff.), but his argument is immediately undercut by the
appearance of Ignatius from hellish depths. For the first time
the conspirators as well as the readers are made to perceive the
true origins of the Plot, and the message is driven home by the
ghastly and unmmistakeably horrid appearance of Nemesis with her
grisly warning for Garnet (answering and parodying the earlier
appearance of the false Hope to Catesby). At the end Satan "kills
those he had previously sustained" (II. 498-9); Winter recognises
the truth of the manifestations of God's anger (II. 545), and all
the conspirators ask for pardon for their "abominable enterprise"
(II. 548).

The poem then ends abruptly. We have no account of the trial
and execution of the prisoners, merely a note that they pay a
just penalty. This very abruptness seems to signal that Campion's
focus is as much on the conspirators' forced recognition of their
guilt and on the sorting out of the "mingle mangle" of their
false religion as it is upon society's retribution exacted for
their crimes. It is this discovery which provides the thematic
momentum of the work, and it is, perhaps, the urgency with which
it is pursued which raises the poem above a merely ornamented
narrative. For in its effort of discrimination it articulates
something of the nervous uncertainty which made it necessary to
turn the events of 1605 into a myth of divine deliverance.

In many ways it is not inappropriate to set this most ambi-
tious Latin poem alongside Campion's masques.   In his court com-
missions of 1607 and 1613 he worked through some of the problems
of articulating pressing contemporary political issues (the Union
of England and Scotland and the marriage of Princess Elizabeth)
in a framework of myth.   Masques work essentially by a technique
of polarisation. The forces of disorder represented in the anti-
masque are routed by the appearance of courtly masquers, specifi-
cally under the tutelage of the monarch in the audience whose
servants they are. This poem, like the masques, is fundamentally
implicated in the mythology of the Stuart court. Like them, also,
it manages to turn the comlexities of political reality into a
readily comprehensible dichotomy. But at the same time the poem,
like the masques, tries to establish some kind of attitude to the
historical events it celebrates, and thus preserve a dynamic
relationship between history and myth.
It is therefore important to recognise that this work is
articulating a political stance which is something more than
inert recapitulation of James's preferred policies. For insofar
as the poem presents a view of events it seems to wish to take a
more firmly anti-Catholic stance than James himself wanted. We
have noted the way in which the memory of Queen Elizabeth is
repeatedly insisted upon in the poem, especially in the speech of
Pia Relligio over her tomb. The effort of much of James's propa-
ganda had been to insist on his own clemency to the Catholics in
contrast to the severity of his predecessor. It is doubly sig-
nificant, therefore, that Campion not only compresses his account
of James's speech to Parliament, but adds a conclusion notably
more bellicose than anything in the published version of the
speech, and puts into James's mouth the words "It is now time to
defend our old laws, not to find new ones" (II. 218-9).   Just as
in The Lord Hay's Masque Campion had used the figure of Diana to
recall the memory of Elizabeth as a gentle rebuke of the King[44]
so it would seem that in this poem he is continually reminding
James of the necessity of his following the religious policies
mapped out by his predecessor. In so doing he was not by any
means unusual - but to recognise this aim in the poem is to give
it the kind of political edge that may be recognised in all of
Campion's panegyric works. Complicit with Stuart ideology they
may be - but within that frame they articulate a coherent politi-
cal stance often somewhat at variance with the preferred policies
of the King. Campion was certainly not one of the more extreme
pro-Protestant, anti-Spanish faction for whom the memory of Queen
Elizabeth acted as a rallying point in their opposition to James.
In The Lord's Masque Campion shows himself to be in sympathy with

the King's desire for peace, as he expresses hopes for the mar-
riage of Princess Elizabeth and Frederick, Elector Palatine, that
are notably temperate. Nonetheless it would seem that for the
poet who wrote memorable elegies on the death of Prince Henry,
and for whom the memory of Elizabeth does have a special place,
James's pacific clemency went too far. In this poem, as in the
masques, he offers advice couched in compliment.

Be that as it may, it seems right to suggest that this poem is
so much more successful than his early attempt to turn the events
of 1588 into an epical poem, precisely because he had learnt,
during his work on the court masques, much more about ways of
negotiating between the matter of history and of myth. This
work, then, makes a very significant contribution to our under-
standing of the side of Campion's work which has traditionally
been neglected in an exclusive concentration on his lyric and
musical art.

David Lindley

The Poem and the Classics

Though Campion writes in Latin in The Gunpowder Plot, he does
not do so as a laudator temporis acti but as a Christian poet
dedicated to greater subjects and higher truths than those known
to pagan antiquity. Here may be noted the dedicatory poem to
James, the reference to the fictions of the Greeks at I. 311 and
to the Delphic oracle at I. 660. Nevertheless allusions to the
ancient world actually constitute the thought and imagery of
these three passages, and in the poem as a whole there is sub-
stantial colouring from classical sources. Most notably, the
whole apparatus of the ancient underworld from Hesiod to Seneca
could very usefully be adapted in the representation of the
unholy workings of Satan and Ignatius. Some of the more obvious
allusions are recorded in the notes.

Of the literary allusions, perhaps the most prominent and the
most pointed, and Campion's readers must have recognised it as
such, is to the story of Iphigeneia as told by Lucretius in his
didactic poem De rerum natura. Here it is an exemplary tale told
to illustrate the iniquitous power of religion, for Agamemnon is
persuaded to sacrifice his daughter by a priest, which leads to
the famous emphatic concluding line:

tantum religio potuit suadere malorum
[so powerful religion has been in persuading to evil deeds].

Campion apostrophises impious religion (I. 127ff.) and goes one
better than Lucretius in giving modern examples of new and
greater iniquity: subject sons can kill their kings, and now it
is honourable to destroy the triple kingdom uno flamine (I. 132).
The word flamen in poetry can be used to mean a "blowing" or
"blast" and so here refers to the single blast of the gunpowder.
But flamen is more commonly known as the standard Latin word for
"priest", so that by a fine stroke of wit Campion lays bare his
own plot.   Rome designs to pervert the triple kingdom through the
agency of a single priest, Garnet, who when consulted by Catesby,
gives positive encouragement to the plotters (I. 362-9).   So much
more ruinous has priestly power become since the time of Lucre-
tius.   In fact Lucretius's conclusion, suitably adapted to his
Protestant cause, could be said to be Campion's starting point as
the false religion at the devil's persuasion (suasore) transmits
its hopes to Catesby in the opening of the argument of Book One.
The allusion is a signal to his readers, if one be needed, that
Campion is approaching his task rather in the manner of Lucre-
tius: the gunpowder plot is an exemplary tale affording a salu-
tary lesson.

Elsewhere Campion rarely alludes directly to particular pas-
sages in quite this way.   Allusions tend to be more general and
sometimes indirect as in the following example. After all has
been revealed, the conspirators are likened to actors in a tragic
play on a Senecan theme, who, when the final horror approaches,
suddenly lose the audience's sympathy and are laughed off the
stage in contempt (II.   230-41). Horrific mythological crimes
involving Hercules, Thyestes and Althea are thus evoked at one
remove: the central point of the comparison stresses failure.
Objects of horror before the denouement, after it the conspira-
tors become pathetic figures when the horrendous design that
threatened so much sound and fury comes to signify nothing.   The
simile may be said to encapsulate Campion's attitude to the con-
spirators and his treatment of them. They are raised in the imag-
ination, only to be reduced.   In the theatrical simile, he clev-
erly subordinates the classical material with which he wishes to
impart a general imagistic colouring by alluding to a contempo-
rary stage experience doubtless familiar to his readers. The con-
temporary note predominates too in all the other extended similes
of which there are about a dozen covering a range of topics from
music to bear-baiting.

There are many verbal echoes of classical originals.   When

Satan marks out Catesby as the chosen man of fate - <u>illum</u> <u>poscere</u>
<u>fata</u> (I. 156) - the phrase is an exact echo of Latinus's recogni-
tion at <u>Aeneid</u>,   VII.   272 that Aeneas is the   stranger fated to
marry his daughter.   When he sees   that all is lost, Catesby in
urging some final effort so that   they should not die unavenged -
<u>sic</u> <u>non</u> <u>moriemur</u> <u>inulti</u>, II.   291 - echoes the famous last words
of Dido,   <u>moriemur</u>   <u>inultae/</u> <u>sed</u>   <u>moriamur</u> [we will die unavenged,
but let us die] at <u>Aeneid</u>, IV. 659.   The irony in the first place
and the inversion in the second   may perhaps be deliberate but in
the majority of Virgilian echoes it   is the general   epic prove-
nance   rather   than a   specific   parallel   or inversion   that   is
intended.   Hope finds Catesby overcome by   sleep and wine - <u>somno</u>
<u>vinoque</u> <u>sepultum</u> (I. 160); the Greeks on Troy's last night invade
the city <u>somno</u> <u>vinoque</u> <u>sepultam</u> (<u>Aeneid</u>, II.   265).   On the night
of the impending disaster the moon   and the stars afford no warn-
ing signs   but continue   in benign silence   - <u>per</u>   <u>amica</u> <u>silentia</u>
<u>vadunt</u> (II.   255);   the Greek fleet returns to   Troy through the
friendly silence   of a   quiet moon -   <u>tacitae</u> <u>per</u>   <u>amica</u> <u>silentia</u>
<u>lunae</u> (<u>Aeneid</u>, II.   255).   Aeneas is guided by his mother Venus
through   the fighting   and   flames of Troy   <u>per</u>   <u>tela</u> <u>per</u>   <u>ignes</u>
(<u>Aeneid</u>, II. 664). Winter reflects that for the Catholic cause he
is prepared to   go through·fire and   sword - <u>per</u> <u>tela</u>   <u>per</u> <u>ignes/</u>
<u>ire</u> <u>juvat</u> (I. 213).   Coming after the projected plot, what other-
wise might   be a   stale metaphor   or epic   cliché has   real point
here.   Elsewhere well worn epic formulae serve their turn,   like
<u>horresco</u> <u>referens</u> [I shudder to tell the tale] (II.   57) and <u>sid</u>-
<u>era</u> <u>testor</u> [the stars be   my witness] (I. 229).   The description
of the dead of night -   <u>tempus</u> <u>erat</u> <u>penitus</u> <u>victis</u> <u>mortalia</u> <u>curis</u>
(II.   25) - is a variation of a Virgilian expression, <u>tempus</u> <u>erat</u>
<u>quo</u> <u>prima</u> <u>quies</u> <u>mortalia</u> <u>aegris</u> (<u>Aeneid</u>,   II. 268).   In the
description of   Ignatius's shade,   the   Latin phrase   <u>olim</u> <u>qualis</u>
<u>erat</u> (II.   353) recalls the   exclamation of Aeneas when Hector's
ghost appears to   him in a dream: <u>ei</u> <u>mihi</u> <u>qualis</u> <u>erat</u> (<u>Aeneid</u>,
II.   274).   Such   echoes,   and these are but a   few,   are almost
inevitable in a neo-Latin writer   using the hexameter,   since all
writers of   Latin verse in   Campion's time   as now are   taught to
regard Virgil as   the model of elegant and⁻ polished Latinity for
imitation and emulation.
    Campion aspired to   cast his story in a   dignified and elegant
style befitting both the gravity of the subject and the personage
to whom it was dedicated, but the result is by no means stiff and
bloodless Virgilian pastiche.   The wit and wordplay that are evi-
dent in the   epigrams are not excluded by an   over delicate sense
of decorum from   the main narrative. (The   invective against the
Jesuits is undertaken with scarcely   disguised relish.) The most

obvious joke, and one that Virgil would never have allowed him-
self is the play on Ignatians and Ignitians, depending on the
Latin ignis meaning "fire" (I. 304-5). But at many points in the
poem Campion's manipulation of the Latin language shows something
more subtle and artful. For example, an element of more refined
wit is apparent at the conclusion of the passage in which the
conspirators' preparations are described. They bring iron imple-
ments in with the powder, put wood on top and with much charcoal
and heaped-up beer barrels they fashion their cellars: cellaria
fingunt (I. 538). Cellarium, a post-classical word meaning "pan-
try" or "store-room", here appropriately suggests the English
word derived from it - "cellars" - but with fingunt meaning "to
fashion or mould" the phrase brings to mind the activity of bees
in making their honeycombs for which cella is the classical word.
This glancing evocation of orderly and fruitful activity serves
to emphasise the grotesque horror of the conspiratorial prepara-
tions and perhaps also underscores the careful and systematic
planning that went into them. Campion's Latin can be rich in
implication.
     There is too in his Latin an economy of expression that is
akin to wit, particularly in relation to a few key words con-
nected with the gunpowder plot.   The full literal and figurative
significance of the words momentum and momen (meaning "a moment
in time", "a movement or upheaval" and "something momentous") is
vividly present in a number of passages (for example: I. 237; I.
415; I. 154; II. 35; II. 176) to suggest in a word what cannot be
brought out fully in translation without excessive paraphrase,
the instantaneous, powerful and momentous effect of the projected
plot.   The most witty and sophisticated example of this economy
is at the climactic moment when Fawkes reveals the "deathly
pile", letiferum cumulum, in the cellar after he has been
detected (II. 46).   The climax is memorable through the wit
whereby cumulus is also used in its figurative sense to convey
the topmost point of Fawkes's audacity, for cumulus as a rhetori-
cal term means "the peroration or climax" of a speech, and the
deadly climax of Fawkes's speech to his amazed captors is that he
would have been prepared to sacrifice himself in the ensuing
conflagration. Other key words connected with the plot are high-
lighted and played upon, such as fulmen, ignis, tonitrua, ictus
and fulgor (see, for example, I. 93; I. 231; I. 497; II. 241; II.
398).   Finally, the wit of the King in solving the riddle of the
letter is second only to the wit of Campion in likening the
quickening of the royal intelligence to the igniting of gunpowder
in a blinding flash when it has been properly primed (I. 671-74).
A neat touch here which cannot be brought out in translation is

the use of <u>recta</u> <u>ratione</u> in the simile where it suggests the
deadly expertise of those who have the know-how to control this
new power corresponding in the main narrative to the right reason
of the King who thwarted this projected blow (<u>ictus</u>) with his
sudden apprehension (<u>ictu</u>), for <u>ratio</u> can mean both "method" and
"reasoning power". It goes without saying that Campion's Latin is
neater and more subtle than any translation can suggest.

These few examples indicate what, sadly, may not be apparent
in the literal and therefore often rather stilted English version
- that Campion's Latin can be lively, interesting and entertain-
ing, and may further suggest that whatever the political or occa-
sional prompting of the poem, The <u>Gunpowder</u> <u>Plot</u> was for its
author no perfunctory exercise in Latin versifying, but an oppor-
tunity to entertain himself and his readers by engaging his ready
wit upon a congenial topic still of contemporary interest.

Robin Sowerby

C

NOTES

1   M. R. James, A Descriptive Catalogue of the Manuscripts in the Library of Sidney Sussex College, Cambridge (Cambridge, 1895) p. 42.
2   Peter Beal, ed., Index of Literary Manuscripts, 5 Vols, I, Part One (London and New York, 1980) pp. 167, 189.
3   See R. C. Bald, John Donne: A Life (Oxford, 1970) p. 539.
4   Leicester Bradner, "References to Chaucer in Campion's Poemata", RES 12 (1936) pp. 322-3.
5   Walter R. Davis, ed., The Works of Thomas Campion (London, 1969), pp. 359-60.
6   See Linda Levy Peck, Northampton: Patronage and Policy at the Court of James I (London, 1982) pp. 110-113. Francis Osborne, in a character sketch prefaced to his play on the Frances Howard marriage and murder, described Northampton, perhaps justly, as one "no farther concerned in religion than it produced profit at home and esteem from abroad", and commented: "His leisure had given him time to rake up so much learning as rendered him no less tedious to the wise than unintelligible to the ignorant, of the truth of which a surfeit may be taken by any that shall read his Gunpowder Treason". The True Tragicomedy Formerly Acted at Court, eds. John Pitcher and Lois Potter, in The Renaissance Imagination, ed. Stephen Orgel, Vol. 3 (New York and London, 1983) p. 13.
7   For Campion's Protestantism as expressed in his First Booke of Ayres see David Lindley, Thomas Campion (Leiden, 1986) pp. 32-3.
8   Milton's In Quintum Novembris is but the best known of the excercises on the subject.
9   See Percival Vivian, Campion's Works (Oxford, 1909) pp. xlii-xlvi, and for discussion of the circumstances as they affected Campion's other works see David Lindley, Thomas Campion, pp. 25-29, 221-30.
10 Vivian, p. xlvii.
11 The Discourse was intitially printed with King James's speech to Parliament, and was later included in his Workes (1616), though it is clearly not of his authorship. It is also to be found bound with some copies of Relation.
12 "Gunpowder Plot and the Politics of Dissent", in Early Stuart Studies, ed. Howard S Reinmuth Jr. (Minneapolis, 1976) p. 110.

13 The memorable phrase is from Stow, Annals (1614 ed.) p. 875.
14 Ralph Winwood, Memorials of Affairs of State (London, 1725) II. 171.
15 See Relation, Sig. S3r-v, and John Speed, History of Great Britaine (1611) p. 892.
16 Relation, Sig. A4r-v.
17 Relation, Sig. F1r.
18 Derek Hirst, Authority and Conflict: England 1603-1658 (London, 1986) p. 84.
19 Carol Z. Weiner, "The Beleaguered Isle. A Study of Elizabethan and Early Jacobean Anti-Catholicism", Past and Present 51 (1971) p. 30.
20 C. H. McIlwain, ed., The Political Works of James I (Cambridge, Mass. and Oxford, 1918) p. 285.
21 "So was this Oath . . . ordained for making a difference betweene the ciuilly obedient Papists, and the peruerse disciples of the Powder-Treason" (McIlwain, p. 75).
22 (?)Richard Broughton, A Iust and Moderate Answer (1606) Sig. A2r.
23 Quoted in Bernard Bassett, The English Jesuits (London, 1967) pp. 2-3.
24 Pseudo-Martyr (1610) p. 143.
25 The controversial works on this subject, and on others relevant to the Gunpowder Plot, are usefully categorised and listed by Peter Milward, in Religious Controversies of the Jacobean Age (London, 1978).
26 Thomas H. Clancy Papist Pamphleteers (Chicago, 1964) p.197.
27 See A. E. Malloch, "Father Garnet's Treatise of Equivocation", Recusant History, 15 (1981) pp. 387-395, and "Equivocation: A Circuit of Reasons", in Familiar Colloquy: Essays presented to Arthur Edward Parker, ed. Patricia Bruckmann (Ottawa, 1978) 132-143.
28 An Answere to Certaine Scandalous Papers (1606) Sig. C3v.
29 The Earl of Salisbury, quoted in Philip Caraman, Henry Garnet (London, 1964) p. 351
30 Malloch, "Treatise of Equivocation", p. 393.
31 see S. R. Gardiner, What Gunpowder Plot Was, Ch. IV.
32 This work was reissued in an enlarged form in 1609; it was translated with the author's approval by A. P. in 1610 as Popish Piety, and again, much dilated, by John Vicars as Mischeefes Mysterie (1617)).
33 BL Royal MS 12.A.LIX
34 See Frederick S. Boas, ed., Giles and Phineas Fletcher, Poetical Works, 2 Vols. (Cambridge, 1908) I, pp. xii-xvii, 97-123.

35   See Benjamin Boyce,   "News from Hell",   PMLA   58 (1943) pp.
      402-37.
36   Davis, ed., The Works of Thomas Campion, p. 64.
37   "The Beleaguered Isle", p. 34.
38   McIlwain, Works of James I, p. 71.
39   "Gunpowder, Treason and Scots", Journal of British Studies 24
      (1985) pp. 141-168.
40   An Answere to Certaine Scandalous Papers, Sig E3r.
41   A very similar collocation of attitudes is found in the work
      of William Fennor, who may aptly be quoted in this study,
      since he is the first known poet from Leeds. In Fennors
      Descriptions (1616), we find:
          Thus a good Prince is by the Angels guarded.
          What Plots were lay'd gainst Queene Elizabeth,
          To cut her off by an vntimely death?
          Yet maugre all their blasted blacke infection
          She liu'd, till heauen cal'd her by election.
          Inioy abounding, and her Princely Throne,
          She left vnto your Maiesty alone:
          Whom God hath placed with a peacefull hand,
          The like hath scarce beene heard in any land;
          To haue so many foes, and all turne friends,
          By th'which the sword of warre, to th'Oliue bends.
      ("A Speech concerning the Gowries treason, and the Gun-Powder
      Plot", Sig. E4v-F1r. I owe this reference to Chris Shepherd,
      Curator of the Brotherton Collection.)
42   A. J. Smith, ed.,   John Donne, The Complete English Poems
      (Harmondsworth, 1971) p. 163
43   Popish Piety, trans. A.P., st. 34.
44   See David Lindley, Thomas Campion, pp. 185-90.

Liber 2.

Argumentum.

Flaucus vt opportunè opera, fatoq̄ prehensus
Cneueti scelus expandit, cameramq̄ secundus
Persequitur liber; excusso noua gaudia somno
Rex placide admittit; tota quæ, luce renata,
Vrbe calent: studio capiendæ fingit Elizæ
Venatum multis Digbæus cinctus amicis.
Vindictam statuit populo acclamante senatus:
Ignati vmbra animos impellit ad arma rebelles.
Conjuratorum fædantur puluere vultus,
Pugna mox cæsiquisunt, captiue sub vmbra.

His vix digestis premit oras Oceani sol,
Mane cui ignaro spectacula quanta parantur,
Quam taciti sceleris plena, et mæroris acerbi?
Sed neq̄ prodigiosi ignes, nec turbinis atri
Insolitus fragor ardentes terrebat equorum
Præcipitantum animos, non fluxum, aut pensile mon=
                                          struum.
Nox tenebris contenta suis et Luna vetustis
Sideribus, nec spectra solo dant, nec noua cælo
Signa sed innocuè per amica silentia vadunt.
Eduntur clausis suspiria nulla sepulchris

Sidney Sussex MS 59: Beginning of Liber 2

Liber 1

Thomae Campiani Londinatis,
D:Med:

De puluerea coniuratione

Libri 2

[Ad augustissimum, serenissimumque Jacobum
magnae Britanniae regem &c.

Querna corona Ioui datur olim, laurea Phoebo,
  Myrtea dulce caput Cypridis vmbra tegit;
Spicea sed Cererem cingunt, hederacea Bacchum
  Serta, decus veteres, sic tribuere deis
Pro meritis cuicunque suum; nec debita facto
  Siqua erat, authori gratia parca fuit.
Coelestes pius hinc mortalibus error honores
  Indulsit, memor et numina fecit amor.
Humano generi gratis neque profuit vllus
  Orbe nouo, Graijs si sit habenda fides.
Quales ergo tibi Rex maxime soluet honores
  Gens Britonum, quasi nunc orbe renata suo?
Quam tua restituit prudentia coelitus orta,
  Seruauitque dolo cum ruitura foret.
Pars ego tam magni populi leuis, hoc tibi struxi
  Laudis opus, cecinit quod pia musa mihi;
Vltima quod maneat precor vsque in secla superstes,
  Hostibus officium triste, salubre tibi.]

Book 1

Thomas Campion of London
D. Med.

On the gunpowder plot

Two books

To his most august and serene majesty James,
King of Great Britain etc.

In time past a crown of oak was accorded to Jove, and one of laurel to Phoebus; myrtle shade covered the sweet head of Cypris; but garlands of corn ears encircled Ceres, wreaths of ivy Bacchus; then the ancients gave the gods their due tribute of honours to each according to his services; nor if there was any debt owed for a particular deed was thanks to its author grudging. Thus pious error conferred heavenly honours on mortal things, and mindful love made divinities. Thus no being was of service to the human race without thanks in the spring time of this earth, if we can trust the Greeks. What sort of honour should the British people, virtually born again in the world, pay to you, O mightiest of kings? Your good wisdom which had its origin in heaven, restored them and saved them when they were about to come to ruin through treachery. An insignificant member of this great people, I have made this work of praise for you, which the faithful muse has sung for me. And may this remain ever living for all generations, I pray, a dutiful gift that brings gloom to the enemy and health and strength to you.

In Iesuitas Epigramma i

Olim neci datis lupis Britannicis
Cum nuspiam pateret exteris locus
Astu superuenere Romani lupi,
Tecti cucullis, deuorant impune oues
Nihil timentes; donec indutus pari
Pastor cucullo clanculum Germanicus
Orbem soporum suscitat, nubem exuit,
Taxans luporum proprio vultu dolos.
His denuo pulsis gregi accedit salus
Antiqua; fraudem Roma sed supplet nouam,
Gentique veste consona vulpes tegit
Furtim irruentes proditorio impetu,
Vanis ferentes horridas caudis faces,
Queis amputatis, tertium Britannia
Canit triumphum; numquid haec vltra potest
Pullo Latinus igne, aut arte Tartarus?

Epigramma 2

Romani veteres tribus fuere
Noti nominibus satis superque,
Sed vix ter totidem, quaterue nosci
Possunt Londonia vrbe Iesuitae.

Epigramma 3

Anglus nomine Iesuita mire
Gaudet multiplici, nouem, decemue
Vsurpat varie, et subinde plura,
Sed ficta omnia, nam suum tacere
Verum falsiloquus cauet perite.
Nunc istam mihi gratiam mereri
Fas sit, nominaque nidere aptiora
Illi quot lubet, esse vel paterno
Quae plus propria nemo denegabit.
Desertor patriae, pudor parentum,
Exul, transfuga, proditor spuendus
Stultorum Dominus, superbientum
Seruus, Romuleae rei veredus,
Hispanus iocus atque sycophanta,

Epigram 1 Against the Jesuits

Once upon a time, after wolves in Britain had become extinct,
Roman wolves, when there was nowhere open to them abroad,
excelled in trickery, as, hidden in hoods, they devour the sheep
with impunity, fearing nothing until a German shepherd clothed in
a similar hood roused the sleepy world, and stripped off the
veil, rating the wiles of the wolves at their proper value. With
these driven out again, the old safety returned to the flock; But
Rome supplies new treachery, and clothes its foxes in a dress
appropriate to their kind; they invade furtively with treacherous
force and carry terrible brands in their vain tails. When these
are cut off Britain celebrates its joy in song for a third time.
Surely the Latin with his black fire, or the Devil with his black
art cannot attempt more?

Epigram 2

The old Romans were perfectly well known by three names, but our
Jesuits in London town can scarcely be known by three or four.

Epigram 3

An English Jesuit wondrously rejoices in many names, and usurps
nine or ten variously and thence more, but all fictitious. For
false speaking he is skilfully careful to keep his real name
quiet. Now may it be right to earn merit for myself, and to
attach as many names as is pleasing more appropriate for that
fellow which no one will deny are more proper than his paternal
name. Deserter of his country, shame of his parents, exile, ren-
egade, despicable traitor, lord of the stupid, servant of the
proud, errand boy of the Roman criminal, Spanish tool and trick-

Sermonis dubij pater, piusque
Mendax, tum generi haud nimis pudicus
Suasor foemineo, cruentus, audax,
Bellorum institor, atque regicida.
Illi haec nomina si sciam placere,
Mox plura adijciam, nec est verendum
Ne non copia suppetat nouorum.

Epigramma 4

Quos vocat haereticis studet Anglis Roma mederi
Puluere nec sancto, nec diacatholico;
Catholicos quamuis et sanctos vendicat vna,
Puluere sed Monachi disdiadaemonico.

Epigramma 5

Alludens ad Ignati conclaue
Ioh:Dun Doct:Theol:

Dun taxat libro Iesuitas non tamen vno
    Duntaxat, lingua ridet at Ausonia;
Ausonia in lingua semel est dun sillaba prima
    Duntaxat, primas Dun vbi taxat habet.

ster, author of ambiguous language, pious fraud, then a none too
chaste charmer of the female sex, bloody, reckless, an instigator
of wars and killer of kings. Soon I shall add more, and it is
not to be feared that there will not be a plentiful supply of new
ones.

Epigram 4

Those from the English heretics whom she calls to herself Rome
wishes to be cured by means of a powder neither holy nor unCa-
tholic. Nevertheless she punishes the Catholics and the holy
together but with a monk's diabolical powder.

Epigram 5

Alluding to <u>Ignatius his Conclave</u>
John Donne, Doctor of Theology

Donne taxes the Jesuits not however in one book
   Simply [when he (Donne) taxes] but he mocks them in the Latin
language;
In the Latin language 'dun' is the first syllable once
   Simply [of duntaxat], when Donne taxes he has more than one
first.
         [when he (Donne) taxes]

Thomae Campiani

de puluerea coniuratione
Liber 1

Argumentum

```
+------------------------------------------------------------+
|  Alma Dei prior acta refert, et Daemonis iras,             |
|  Spes sua suasore hoc falsa est a relligione               |
|  Missa Catisbaeo, socios is conuocat, et rem               |
|  Pulueream inducit, consultusque approbat illam            |
|  Garnetus, Faucum transmittit Belgia, coeptis              |
|  Qui fossis praeit; hinc ad busta precatur Elizae          |
|  Flens pia relligio, coeli cui subuenit ales;              |
|  Temporaque indicti sunt interrupta senatus.               |
|  Littera Monteglo datur, hanc rex discutit, inde           |
|10| Pulueris exponens, cui jussa est cautio, technam.       |
+------------------------------------------------------------+
```

      Patroni magnum cano, mirum opus omniponentis
Dulce salutiferum; quantum non praestitit olim
Cum fidit exulibus mare, pronosque obruit hostes;
Quantum non Solymae infestas cum dispulit vno
Ingentes acies ictu super astra triumphans.
Hoc solo minus esse iuuat, cui [maxima cedunt;]
Scilicet vnigenae charo cum sanguine fuso,
[Et victa sibi morte deus reuocauerat orbem.]
      Tu tua celsa mihi ter maxime facta canenti
20   Adde animum, mentique aciem, de pectore curas
Pelle graues, oculisque obiectas discute nubes;
Inferni reserem intrepidus scelera alta tyranni
In terram immeritam, atque tuam; noua dira nefanda,
Horrida [diuini sub cultus nomine coepta.]
      O miseram, o nullam prope magna Britannia gentem
Ni respexisset pater optimus, atque ruenti
Diuinum auxilium nullo metuente tulisset.
Illius aeterno celebremus carmine munus,
Omnis posteritas memori quod mente reuoluat.
30   Humani generis vetus, et non flexilis hostis,
Vmbrarum dominus, [summi semperque colendi
Numinis inuisor, iucundae lucis et osor,
Versutus, vanus, nulli non] fomes, et author
Dissidio (multum fletae post funus Elizae
Pacifico tandem sceptro cedente monarchae

Thomas **Campion**

On **The Gunpowder Plot**
Book One

The Argument

The first book relates the bountiful acts of God, and the anger
of the devil, at whose persuasion the false religion transmits
its hopes to Catesby; he calls his comrades together and broaches
the gunpowder plot; Garnet is consulted and approves of it; Bel-
gium sends across Fawkes who superintends the beginning of the
tunnelling; thereupon True Religion offers tearful prayers before
the tomb of Elizabeth; a winged messenger from heaven comes to
her aid; the times of the appointed assembly are postponed; a
letter is given to Monteagle; the King, to whom the task of tak-
ing precaution has been decreed, deciphers the letter, thence
exposing the device of the powder.

I sing the mighty and wondrous work of the all powerful pro-
tector, sweet and saving; which was not more pre-emininent in
that day when he divided the waters of the sea for the exiles and
overwhelmed their enemies as they rushed forward, or when he
routed the mighty forces of Solyman with a single blow triumphant
above the stars. It is his pleasure that it is less only than
that before which even the greatest things yield, namely the time
when, the precious blood of the only begotten shed and death van-
quished, God had recalled the world to himself.
Do thou give to me as I sing your lofty deeds, thrice great
God, spirit and a discerning sharpness of mind, dispel heavy
cares from my heart, scatter the clouds that impede my sight, let
me relate fearlessly the high crimes of the infernal power
against the undeserving earth that is yours, new terrible abomi-
nations, fearful deeds begun under the pretext of reverence for
God.
O your wretched race, mighty Britain, O almost null and void,
if God in his great goodness had not had regard for you and
brought divine aid to you on the road to disaster though no one
was afraid. His benevolence we celebrate in eternal song which
all posterity will call to mind.
The old intractable enemy of the human race, the lord of the
underworld, who envies the supreme power that is ever to be wor-
shipped, the hater of sweet light, crafty, vain, kindler and
author of every dissension (when the sceptre of peace after the
death of the much lamented Elizabeth at length duly yields to her

Iure suo) vt primum firmatas vndique vidit
Res Britonum dubias, oleaque per omnia pacem
Ire coronatam, templis accrescere sacros
Cultus, laetitiam siluis resonare, decusque
40   Multiplici pompa replere palatia et vrbes;
Nil prodesse dolos, sancto se sternere regi
Nequidquam insidias; vltro jam ponere suetas
Hesperios jras, [sociasque extendere dextras;
Nunc et Hybernorum requiescere conscia tela,]
Nullum adeo superesse locum crepitantibus armis,
Seu tacitae fraudi; sensit mox Tartareus vim
Coelestem, nec enim sine numine talia fiunt,
Impius ergo tremit, simul et fremit ore canino
Diras eructans, et coelum voce lacessit.
50   Nec mihi fas ait, o superi, nec denique cordi est
Aurea stelliferi tolli ad laquearia coeli,
Lucentesque domos, vobis [sublimia] habete,
Imperium terrestre, et nigri jura profundi
Nolite inuidisse mihi, nec numina vestra
Immiscete meis rebus, lucemue tenebris.
Nonne odium regina meum matura sepulchro
Condidit illaesum corpus, celebrata trophaeis
Magnificae pacis populo post fata relictae
Multum dilecto, multo dilectior ipsa?
60   Quidue mihi toties mors exoptata deinde
[Profuerit defunctae] hostis? nouus ecce superstes
Imminet huic capiti infestus magis, atque tremendus,
Quo magis instructus mentem est coelestibus armis.
Vestrum opus o superi, vestrum est hoc omne, nec intra
Tanta cadunt animi humani miracula vires.
Heu quantas frustra fabricas admouimus? haerent,
Semper et herebunt vestro sub tegmine tuti
Numen qui norunt misere lenire precando.
Diuorum ergo mihi merito est inuisa potestas,
70   Lux odio, et coelum est, et pulchri quicquid vterque
Sustinet axe polus: verbis nec supplicat vltra
Impurus daemon, celeri ferit astra boatu,
Ingentesque globos tenebrarum montibus aequos
Aerata jaculare manu, tegere aethera nube,
Et quantum ex jra potuit confundere mundum.
Formas mille subit monstrosas, mille Chimaeras
Insano simulat vultu, nunc tortilis anguis
Reptat, nunc sursum volitat draco, mox fremit vrsus,
Tartara mox lupus impensis vlulatibus vrget,
80   Taurus et horrendum mugit modo cornua vibrans,

successor) as soon as he saw the once doubtful affairs of Britain
now settled and peace going olive-crowned through all the realm,
sacred worship on the increase, joy resounding in the woods, cit-
ies and palaces replete with splendour in varied pomp, seeing
that tricks were no longer any use, treachery had prostrated
itself to the holy king in vain, that the Irish now of their own
accord suppressed their wonted hostility and extended the hand of
friendship, that the conspiring arms of the Scots were quiet and
that there was no place left for the clank of armour or for
secret guile, the devil soon felt the force of heaven, nor did
such things come to pass without God's will; the impious one
therefore trembles, at the same time he gnashes his doglike jaws,
belching out furies, and assails heaven with his cry:

"It is not permitted for me, powers above," he says, "nor is
it ultimately my desire to be raised to the golden roof of the
starry heavens; keep your halls of light and things sublime to
yourselves. Do not begrudge me dominion over the earth and
rightful rule of the dark abyss nor mix your power in my affairs,
or light in the dark. Surely the queen has buried her hatred for
me in the ripeness of the tomb, her inviolate corpse much cele-
brated with trophies for a magnificent peace bequeathed after her
death to a much loved people, much more beloved herself? What
shall the death so often desired of my dead foe then have prof-
ited me? Behold a new surviving adversary threatens danger to
this head, and is more to be feared as he is more equipped in
mind with heavenly armour. This is your work, powers above, this
is all yours, nor do such great marvels fall within the power of
the human spirit. Alas what great stratagems do we move in vain?
They who know how to mollify your power by cringing prayer stand
fast, and and always will stand fast, safe under your protection.
Therefore justly hateful to me is the power of the gods, light,
heaven, and all the beauty either pole sustains on its axis."

The unholy spirit does not humble himself more in words, he
strikes the stars with a swift roar, hurls from his brazen hand
mighty globules of dark shade equal to mountains, covers the air
in cloud and confounds the world as much as he could through
anger. He assumes a thousand monstrous shapes and imitates in
his maddened visage a thousand Chimaeras, now he creeps a writh-
ing snake, now upwards flies like a dragon, then growls like a
bear, then as a wolf menaces Hell with urgent howlings, now shak-
ing his horns he roars terribly as a bull, now a savage wild boar

Trux modo frendet aper; species tunc vndique miscet
Immanes, quicquid truculenti est arte nefanda
Vt sibi conciuit pallentes territat vmbras.
Sed fesso immodicus simul aestus corde quieuit
Ecce cucullatus reliquis audentior ipsum
Alloquitur daemon, ne te supreme patrone
Romanae causae plus aequo cura ruentis
Tangat quid populo si res modo tota patescit
Lutheri inuidia? mitra nil notius? esto;
90   Paucorum manibus patrari magna solebant,
Et nisi mens laeua est, etiam nunc maxima possunt.
Se Britones tutos maris intra moenia jactant,
Et procul irrident Romana tonitrua, fulmen
Attamen inuita cogentur voce fateri.
Sunt, pater, addictae summis conuentibus aedes
Antiquae, quas rex proceresque subire statuto
Assensere die, et melioris portio populi;
Has simul impletae sunt vno dirue flatu,
Sulphureus tibi puluis adest, ignisque sepultus,
100 Inuentum hoc nostrum est, talesque creatur in vsus.
Consilium inferno placet, authorisque coronat
Cupresso rasum caput, omine laetus vterque est.
        Compertum esse duas jamdudum est relligiones;
Altera de Coelo in terras descendit, amica
Pacis, inops cultus, humilis, tamen ore decoro,
Constantique animo et vultu: comes assidet illi
Ingenuus metus, et spes vsque erecta, futurae
Laetitiae praesaga, et semper conscia veri.
Lusca sed ex caecis auri est emissa fodinis
110 Altera, celsa, minax, presso insidiosaue fastu,
Expers natiui decoris, fuco sibi formam
Concilians, varijs, vanisque ornata lapillis.
Seruilis sequitur pauor hanc, incertaque gressus
Ebria spes, audax tamen; alti in vertice montis
Splendescit speciosa domus, distinctaque pictis
Turribus, exterius quamuis venerabilis, intus
Horrida spectanti est: stant mille et mille deorum
Postibus effigies referentes ora ferarum,
Daemonaque, et quicquid pauor, atque insania finxit;
120 Dimidium haud capiunt centum capitolia, centum
Vix fando aequabunt tonsores, totue cuculli.
Appositam diris altaribus Iphianissam
Cernere erit misere flentem, patrisque vocantem
Necquicquam auxilium, solus licet imperet, astus
Praeualet irati vatis, cadit hostia ventis,

he gnashes his teeth; then he mingles monstrous shapes on all
sides. As he stirred up for himself through his black art every
form of savagery, he afflicts the pale ghosts with terror. But
as soon as the uncontrolled outburst in his weary heart went
quiet, behold a hooded devil bolder than the rest addressed him:
     "Sovereign protector, are you not more concerned for the
Roman cause threatened with ruin if everything becomes known to
the people through the malice of Luther? Is nothing to be more
notorious than a bishop's mitre? So be it; great things were once
accomplished by the hands of a few, and if there is no ill dispo-
sition, even now the greatest are still possible. The Britons
boast that they are safe within their sea walls and mock Roman
thunder that is far off, nevertheless they will be compelled to
acknowledge a thunderbolt with unwilling voice. There are,
father, ancient chambers for the highest councils to which the
king and the lords have agreed to go on a fixed day, together
with a portion of the better people. As soon as the chambers are
full, destroy them in one blast; the sulphurous powder and buried
fire are ready for you. This is our invention, and is made for
such purposes."
     The advice pleases the devil, and he crowns the shaven head
of its author with cypress, and both rejoice in the token.
     It has long been known that there are two religions. One
came down onto the earth from Heaven, the friend of peace, lack-
ing in artifice, humble, yet with a beautiful face. She is of
unchanging spirit and countenance; in her train is innocent fear,
and hope ever alive, prophetic of future joy and always conscious
of the truth. But the other was sent one-eyed from dark mines of
gold, lofty, threatening, or untrustworthy through hidden pride,
having no natural grace, procuring a beautiful appearance through
disguise, embellished with gems many and vain. A slavish dread
follows in her train and hope that is drunken and of uncertain
step, yet daring. On the top of a high mound glitters a splendid
palace adorned with decorated towers; although on the outside it
is awesome, within it is horrible to look at: there stand on
posts thousands upon thousands of images of gods that suggest the
faces of wild beasts and devils, and every form that dread and
madness has fashioned; a hundred temples could hardly contain
half, and a hundred barbers or as many monks will only with dif-
ficulty be equal to telling the tale of them. Placed on the ter-
rible altars it will be possible to see Iphigeneia weeping
wretchedly and calling vainly for help from her father; though he
alone has command, the cunning of the angry priest prevails, the
sacrificial victim falls to the winds which her father is placat-

D

Quos placat, toto sed vix ita sanguine vatem.
Heu quantum sceleris peragis, quantum inuehis orbi
Impia relligio? sed et haec leuia esse fatemur,
Ludicraque, improbitas primo quae prodidit aeuo,
130   Nostra praeut noua quae fert, atque instructior aetas
Quodcunque in facinus; natos occidere reges,
Iamque vno triplicem peruertere flamine gentem
Suaue et honorificum est: vae vae tibi turbida Roma
Dedecus Imperij, atque animorum peruaga pestis.
Vestibuli ad laeuum patet ingens porticus, auro
Argentoque insignitis suspensa columnis:
Turget jmaginibus locus, expressique resurgunt
Pontifices triplo diademate, vesteque picta
Vsque a Bon'facio, duce quo noua Roma triumphat.
140   Sanctorum necnon statuis, [stultisque tumescit]
Relliquijs, quales in risum, aut vertere possunt
Totum te Heraclite, in fletum aut fundere totum.
Hic se delectat, multum hic dea lusca moratur,
Hic Erebi rex aggreditur sua dira precantem
Teutonicae fidei, Batauisque, pijsque Britannis.
Tartareum vt vidit, cupide mox applicat eius
Dicto aurem, exponit stygius de puluere totam
Ordine rem, coeptis tam tetris esse colore
Multo opus ornatam mittat spem poscit, vt vrat
150   Voce Catisbaeum, caedisque incendat amore:
Stare animo in patriam auerso, rerumque nouarum
Imprimis auido; Grantam illi, aptumque Rucodem
Omnibus in rebus sociosque, paresque futuros.
Vinterum, Vritumque, et te nequissime Perci
Ex notis esse, et causae communis amicis:
Illum tentandum premit, illum poscere fata;
Assensum est, spes festinat meretricia, picta,
Cultaque amatori conductum nobile scortum
Vt solet; aede sua scelerosum sorte sinistra
160   Inuenit oppressum, somno vinoque sepultum,
Lambethi, formosa tuas prope Thamisis vndas;
Surge ait, heu misere dormis (mi dulcis alumne)
Nec te Roma mouet per te male prodita, per te,
Segnitiemque tuam; quod si haec aliena videntur,
Fortunis succurre tuis, auerte ruinam
Luxuries quam festinat, legesque minantur.
Aude aliquid saltem quod spem non fallere possit,
Scis vbi [totius regni est conuentus habendus,]
Idque breui; subtus congesto dirue gentem
170   Puluere fulmineo inuisam; sic victor abibis,

ing, but it is the priest whom he can scarcely placate with her
lifeblood itself. Alas how much wickedness are you bringing to
pass, how much are you oppressing the world, impious religion?
But we bear witness that what evil was brought to light in former
times is trivial and ridiculous in comparison with the novelties
perpetrated by our time, better instructed to every crime.   Sub-
ject sons kill their kings, and now it is sweet and honourable to
destroy the triple kingdom in one blast.   Woe, woe is you, sedi-
tious Rome,   scandal of earthly power and ubiquitous plague of
souls.   To the left of the entrance hall opens out a huge arcade
supported by columns decorated with silver and gold.   The place
is packed with images, and the popes, prominent with triple crown
and with decorated robes, rise again all the way from Boniface
under whose generalship a new Rome triumphs. Likewise it abounds
with statues of the saints and with foolish relics such as could
turn you, Heraclitus, wholly to laughter or plunge you wholly in
tears.   Here the one-eyed goddess delights herself and lingers
long.   Here the king of Hell approaches her who pours down her
dread curses upon the German faith, upon the Dutch and upon the
faithful Britons. When she sees the Infernal One, straightway
she eagerly bends her ear to his words. The Stygian expounds the
whole gunpowder plot from the beginning; such dark undertakings
need much colouring; he demands that she send an extravagant
hope, and that she inflame Catesby with her own voice, and fire
him with love of slaughter.   Catesby has a mind ill disposed to
his country and eager above all for revolution; Grant and Rook-
wood who are compliant with him in all matters are to be his
equals and comrades.   Winter, Wright, and you most reprobate
Percy are notables and friends of the common cause.   He urges
that Catesby be put to the test, and that it is him the fates are
calling.   It is agreed.   Hope hastens seductively on her way,
painted and decked out as a high born harlot is wont to go to her
lover on hire.   She finds the wicked man in his house, weighed
down by his own ill-starred lot, overcome by sleep and wine, at
Lambeth, near your waves, O beautiful Thames.
    "Arise", (she says),"alas, do you sleep in misery my dear
protegé, and does not Rome move you, betrayed by you and your
sloth?   But if this seems the concern of others, rescue your own
fortunes, avert the disaster which your indulgence hastens and
the laws threaten.   Dare something at least which cannot cheat
hope.   You know where the assembly of the whole kingdom is to be
held, and that shortly; destroy the hated people with powder and
fire from below. Thus you will come away victorious, you will be

Clarus et Ausonios inter numerabere diuos.
Dixit, et in tenebras leuis euanescit opacas
Structis insidijs: praecordia concutit horror
Dura Catisbaei, surreptaque turbat imago.
Multa aegro voluente animo, vt lux reddita terris,
Conuocat vnanimes et proditionibus aptos,
Quos bene cognouit, Vinterum pectore fidum
Improbo, et Vritum; solito sed tardior ipsis
Congressis tandem trepidante superuenit aestro
180 Percius, et quid, ait, semper loquimurne sodales,
Nil agimus? regem interimi numquid iuuat ipsum?
En vobis hic certa manus. Sic excipit illum
Ore Catisbaeus blaeso tamen ad mala prompto;
Iamdudum hoc agimus Perci, nobis vt agamus
Dignum aliquid, factis praeeant sed verba necesse est,
Cernendis veluti debentur lumina rebus.
Perdere tam multa sibi prole superstite regem,
Res non digna satis tanta fortissime dextra est,
Ad maiora tibi vigeat dum prouocat vsus.
190 Ingens coeptum animus mi parturit, artis iniquae
Non nihil argutans, fructum sin respicis, vnum est.
Quod decus antiquum templis, animisque piorum
Oppressis requiem certo promittere possit.
Quicquid id est, clamant, fidis ne credere cesset
Auribus, et paribus per cuncta pericula votis.
      Quandoquidem vestris sic illud mentibus, inquit,
Perplacitum est, paucis quod multa requirit, habete.
Ipsum cum populo regem prolemque senatu
Tollere consilium est [simul atri pulueris ictu.]
200   Horrescunt omnes dicto, sanguisque loquentis
Deseruit vultus, communis pallor honesta
Inuitis licet, et diuturna silentia mandat.
Ac veluti varia cum coepta est cantio voce
Condita ad aequales, ex illis forsitan vna
Discors vox strepitu reliquas abrumpit amaro,
Auersata omnesque soni feritate quiescunt.
Haud aliter siluere audito nomine tantum
Pulueris horribili vastantis cuncta tumultu.
      Post longam dubio sic replicat ore quietem
210 Vinterus, non si tellus mihi tota dehiscat,
Omnis et inferni in memet conuertitur horror,
Abstineam si Roma vocat; si [cogat auitae]
Aurea libertas [fidei]; per tela, per ignes
Ire juuat; nec magna metu consulta retracto.
Sed via difficilis, dumetisque obsita terret,

famous and numbered among the gods of Ausonia."

She spoke, and lightly vanishes into the impenetrable shades, the plot now laid. Dread fear shakes the hard heart of Catesby, and the false image throws him into confusion. Turning these things over in his sickened mind, when light was restored to earth, he calls together those of like mind, and those disposed to plotting whom he knew well, Winter trusty in his wicked heart and Wright, but slower than the rest to join their number came Percy, quivering with his customary passion.

"Why" (he says) "do we always talk together as confederates, but do nothing? Do you recall our resolve that the king himself be killed? Behold, here is a resolute hand."

Catesby thus followed him with a stammering tongue, but one nevertheless prompt to ill.

"We have been acting like this for a long time, Percy, so that we may accomplish something worthy of us, but it is necessary that words come before deeds, just as light is necessary for things to be seen. To destroy the king with so many of his offspring left alive is not an exploit sufficiently worthy of so great courage, mightiest of men. May your right arm keep its vigour for greater things until occasion calls for its use. Insistently advocating some deed of inordinate enterprise, my mind conceives a mighty undertaking - if you are looking for a fruitful outcome there is one thing which can with certainty give our places of worship their ancient glory and to the souls of the faithful departed give peace."

Whatever it is, they call upon him not to cease to trust faithful ears and those who have sworn to be one through all perils.

"Since your minds are so greatly pleased with the idea" (he says) "hear in brief what needs much to accomplish. The plan is to remove the king himself and his offspring together with the people and the lords all in a blast of gunpowder."

All grow fearful at his word, and the blood drained from the speaker's face and even in spite of themselves the common fear commands a long and fitting silence. And just as when singing has begun with a variety of sounds come together in harmony, from them perhaps one discordant voice breaks through the rest with a harsh sound, and all become silent, shunning the uncouthness of the noise; in the same way did they grow silent, merely hearing the mention of gunpowder devastating all in a terrible upheaval. After a long silence Winter thus muses in doubtful tones:

"Not even if the whole earth were to open at my feet and the terror of the Infernal One converge upon me, should I hold back if Rome calls; if priceless freedom for our ancient faith necessitates, I would willingly go through sword and fire, nor do I draw back from these mighty resolutions through fear. But the way is difficult and overgrown with thickets, the prospect terri-

Atque bonae male re cedente calumnia causae.
Praeterea nostrum pereunti candida turbae
Pars conserta cadet non contemnenda, cruentis
Ne nimis inuidiosa etiam victoria fiat.
220   Increpat hunc primo diuellens vltima verba
Percius, o nimium exclamat, nimiumque beati,
[Relligioni tot secum mala, tot morientes]
Queis auferre datur discrimina, totque ruinas:
Quam lubet explere hunc numerum, factoque vouere
Tam pulchro hanc animam; tota cum stirpe parentes
Sic misti intereant potius, vindicta profanis
Quam non contingat tam [digna et nobilis, vsu]
Iustitiaque omnes superans [quibus imbuit] aures
Fama meas: nam quid magis aequum, sydera testor,
230   Nos ijsdem quam caede locis vlciscier hostes,
In vitas quibus et fortunas fulmina nostras
Mittere pro libito, nullo cohibente, solebant
Vi decretorum sub auarae nubibus artis?
His liquido acclamat dictis Vritus, et effert
Laudibus authorem, technamque stupescere gestit
Sulphurei cineris, nil certius omnia turbis
Momento immiscere, nouis seu motibus ansam
Posse dare, aut veterem fidei languentis honorem
Spem restaurandi fessis renouare Britannis:
240   Impia sic portenta animo pietatis obumbrant.
Pergite quo properatis ait Vinterus, iniquum
Aequum, si vobis id visum est haud moror, ibo
Quo nos cunque trahunt communia fata, recedat
Pectore nunc omnis pietas in memet, et omnes;
Dispereat quisquis facti successibus obstat.
At sapiens leni primum medicamini Cous
Tentandos morbos docet, id si iuuerit, vltra
Nil opus est, quod si facilis medicina fefellit,
Maiori pugnat, ferro in mala tanta, vel igne.
250   Si placet hunc imitemur, et aduenientis Iberi
Oremus legati operam, si flectere possit
Duri in nos animum regis quos abdicat, vt jus
In patria commune velit concedere terra,
Ac libertatem [sacrorum, O Roma, tuorum.]
Belgarum remoratur adhuc Hispanus in oris
Quo propero, fidum mox conuenturus Oenum,
Charum principibus, nostris et rebus amicum.
Tentandi dubiam, si quid promittere possit,
Legati Hesperij [mea sit] prouincia mentem:
260   Quae mihi pro votis si non successerit, vltra

fies, and if the affair goes badly there is ill repute for our noble cause. Besides, a fair portion of our persuasion will fall with the perishing throng, and that is not to be taken lightly, lest even victory may become too hateful to those who have been too bloody."

Percy rebukes him, first tearing into his last words:

"O much blessed" (he exclaims) "much blessed are those to whom it is given in dying for their religion to remove so many ills, so many dangers and so many devastations. How pleasing to fill up this number and to devote one's soul to so fine a deed. May parents thus die in the company of their whole offspring rather than that so deserved and righteous a vengeance should not fall upon the profane, surpassing all that fame has brought to my ears in its justice and value. For what could be more just - the stars be my witness - than that we should wreak vengeance upon our enemies with death in those same places from which they were accustomed, on the pretext of our greed and craft, to send their thunderbolts against our lives and fortunes by violence of decree at their whim when there was no one to restrain them?

Wright plainly acclaims these words, and heaps their author with praises, and excitedly marvels at the cunning device of the sulphurous dust, reflecting that nothing is more certain to throw everything into confusion in a moment, and either to give occasion to revolution or renew hope of restoring their languishing faith to its old glory among the weary Britons. Thus under the guise of pious intention do they cloak their monstrous impiety.

"Proceed with what you are intent upon," (says Winter) "good, bad, if it seems right to you I have no objection; I will go anywhere our common fate draws us. Now let every pious scruple retreat from me and from all. Perish the man who stands in the way of the success of our enterprise. But the wise doctor from Cos teaches that sicknesses must first be treated with gentle medicine; if that will help, there is no need of anything beyond, but if the easy medicine has failed, he fights with more powerful remedy against such great ills, with steel or fire. If it is acceptable to you, let us imitate him and beg aid from the Spanish envoy who is just now arriving, to see if he can move the mind of the King, hard set against us whom he renounces, to concede to us common rights in our country and freedom for your rites, O Rome. The Spaniard still tarries on Belgian shores, to which I hasten, soon to meet up with our trusty Owen, one who is dear to those in power and a friend to our cause. Let mine be the task of trying out the uncertain mind of the Spanish envoy to see if he can promise anything. If I do not meet with any suc-

Progrediamur, et extremos redeamus ad ignes.
Recte Vinterus sapit, et bene consulit, infit
Percius, at vereor nimium ne frigida spes sit,
Proposito insistat tamen, haec sententia nostra est.
Ista Catisbaeus nil contra, sedulus vrget
Vt peragat Vinterus iter, tum si quid Oenus
Possit id imprimis videat, post illa secutum
Castra diu Austriaco popularem sub duce Faucum
Conueniat, profugumque ad littora nota reducat.
270   Caetera si nil proficiunt, et ad vltima ventum est,
Non fidendum operi [gnarus ni accesserit artis]
Quae praeeat fossis, et caecos dirigat ignes.
Aedes curet ait prope fundamenta senatus
Percius, vt quocunque vacent pretio, ipse satelles
Regius [haud aegre proprios] suadebit in vsus
Cedere, sat numero cum sint, aulaeque propinquae.
Puluis at his nostris ampla vt sit mole paratus
Id mecum Vritus percaute munus obibit,
Vnde scaphis tuto transferri singula possint.
280   Conuenit vt subeant partita negotia, natae
Sed jus suspitioni aliquod ne forte relinquant,
Commissi arcani dant juramenta tacendi
Mutua, et vberius quo res noua credita crescat,
[His sacrum coenale superstitione tumentes]
Adnectunt, et opem vanis conatibus orant.
Proh pudor, et coelum spectant, ipsumque bonorum
Fontem, auersoremque mali, quo vindice solo
Plectitur omne nefas, demens audacia partem
Tam foedi in sceleris vocat, appellantque Iehouam
290   Non nunc vt testem, funestis sed caput ausis.
        His ita compositis, nigri dominator Auerni
De grege daemonico spatiosis eligit alis
Vmbram, qua non est pernicior altera, sed nec
Doctior humanos volitando fallere visus;
Imperat huic dorso Vinterum vt tollat opaco
Quoquo tendit iter, propereque per aethera vectet.
Nec mora sublati superant haud segnius Euris
Substratum mare, et optato potiuntur Oeno.
Crescenti interea conducit Percius aedes
300   Addictas sceleri, quod, vt omnis scrupulus absit,
Ore Catisbaeus sacro studet esse probatum.
        Ordo sacerdotum nouus est qui nomen Iesu
Priuatim vsurpant, erat his Ignatius author,
Vnde Ignatistae dicti melioribus annis,
At nunc Ignistae, merito quod nomen ab igne

cess in my entreaties, let us go further forward, and resort to
the extremity of fire."

"Winter shows good sense and counsels rightly",   begins
Percy, "but I fear very much that the hope is cold.   Neverthe-
less, let him press on with his proposal. This is my mind."

Catesby has nothing against this, and eagerly urges that
Winter undertake his journey: if Owen can offer anything then
let him first look into that, then let him meet our comrade
Fawkes, who for a long time has followed a soldier's life under
the Austrian command, and bring the exile back to his native
shores. If everything else bring no profit, and it has come to
the ultimate, no one is to be entrusted to the task unless he
comes with knowledge of the art of tunnelling and can direct the
unseen fires.

"Let Percy" (he says) "procure for whatever price it takes
buildings near the foundations of the chamber that may be empty -
ones which the king's officer himself will not urge for his own
use, although they be numerous and near the halls. But Wright
will make careful provision with me that there may be powder
ready in sufficient quantity for our purposes from which small
amounts can safely be transferred little by little in boats".

It is agreed how they are to approach their shared tasks,
but so that there should be no chance of their leaving any just
cause of suspicion growing, they swear mutual oaths that their
secret enterprise be kept silent; and so that their new found
confidence together might grow more fruitfully they add to their
oaths, as they swell in superstitious pride, the sacred commun-
ion, and pray for help in their vain endeavours. For shame, they
look to heaven and to the very fountain of all good who turns all
evil aside, by whom, our sole vindicator, the whole abomination
is punished; their insane audacity calls him to a share of so
foul a crime, and they call upon Jehovah not now as a witness but
as the source of their deadly enterprises.

When the conspiracy had come thus far, the lord of dark
Avernus chooses from his flock of devils a shade with spacious
wings than which there is no other more swift, but none more
skilled in deceiving human sight in its flight. He orders the
shade to raise Winter darkly on its back and to convey him
quickly through the air to whatever place he directs his way.
There is no delay; raised aloft they fly above the sea below not
more slowly than the East winds and gain the wished for presence
of Owen. Meanwhile Percy hired buildings suitable for the crime
now taking shape, which, so that every scruple might vanish, Cat-
esby eagerly claimed had been approved by the word of God.

There is a new order of priests which privately usurps the
name of Jesus. Ignatius was their founder, whence they were spo-
ken of as Ignatians in better years, but now "Ignitians" - which

Puluereo traxere sibi: Tagus aureus hydram
Edidit hanc, facie pulchram satis, atque decoram
Intuitu primo, verum si lumina cautus
Acrius infigas, nil turpius, horridiusue
310   Infamis Lernae tulit vnquam foeta veneni
Faex vel Auernales, Graijs fingentibus, vndae.
Visceribus technas, haec monstra, incendia, caedes,
Cultra, venena, tumultus, et non justa recondunt
Bella; nec hos regio serpentes vna coercet,
Omnes quin circumuolitent pernicibus alis
Caecam in perniciem, non speratamque ruinam.
Pax miluis, Iouis alitibus nam retia tendunt;
Nec timidae ceruae, [sed dente ac vngue] leoni
[Spreto] natiuis nunc insidiantur in antris.
320   Sancta cohors Stygio longe gratissima regi
Digna bonis docet esse viris mendacia, menti
Verbaque jurantem contraria cudere linguam.
Heu qualis probitas, heu quam noua, quamque stupenda?
Patribus haud dubie nostris incognita, simplex
Aetas illa fuit prior, indulgentior orbem
Iam pater aethereus maiori lumine lustrat.
Tristis in hanc pestem stabilitur Pyramis olim
Gallica, quae simul est sublata, Henrice peristi,
Bellorum nec te clarissima fama tuorum,
330   Non armata satellitij vis, jamque propinquae
Viribus inconcussae acies potuere tueri
Vnius a vili dextra, ferroque cruento.
Non ita mille dolis licet, insidijsque petita,
Concidit aeterni cura ingens patris Elizae;
Illa fide nunquam defecit, sed cita nantes
Visit Iberorum turres, ac denique vicit
Freta pijs precibus, coelique potentibus armis:
Festinata proin sua classis ne cadat, illi
Aethera pugnabant, fretaque, aligeraeque phalanges.
340   Iamque Ignistarum, solis Garnetus, at Anglis
Praeses agendorum jus clam determinat, ipsi
Quaqua affluxuris citra mare (Belgia sacrae
Cresselli obsequitur, Baldini Hispania voci)
Quanto annis grauior, tanto iste tenebrio doctas
Promptior in fraudes, arcana ac publica nouit,
Et personata didicit pietate juuentam
Ludere, dementesque animas anuumque, senumque.
Rure habitat vacuo, procul urbe, senique ministrat
Pulchra domo plena, et generosae foemina stirpis,
350   Nec desunt homini timidae solatia vitae.

name they have deservedly drawn to themselves from igneous sulph-
ur.   Golden Tagus brought forth this serpent, beautiful enough
in its visage, and splendid on a first glance, but if you care-
fully fix your eyes on it more keenly, then nothing more hideous
or more revolting did that infamous swamp at Lerna full of poi-
son, or the waves of Avernus in the fables of the Greeks ever
bring forth.   These monsters hide in their vitals cunning traps,
burnings, killings, knives, poisons, upheavals and unjust wars;
nor does one area contain these serpents from flitting around on
their swift pinions causing unlooked for disasters and unexpected
ruin.   They are at one with kites, for they stretch their nets
for the birds of Jove; and not for the fearful hind but for the
lion do they now lie in ambush in their very caves, scorning
tooth and claw.   This holy troop, for long most pleasing to the
Stygian king, teaches that there are deceptions worthy of good
men, and teaches the tongue as it swears to forge words that are
opposite to the mind's intention.   Alas, what sort of morality,
alas, how new, and how marvellous?   To our fathers it was, with-
out a doubt, unknown: that former time was simple. Now the ether-
ial father with more indulgence illumines the world with greater
light.   Once the unlucky French Pyramid stood steadfast against
this plague, and as soon as it was ousted, you, Henry, perished;
not the most far flung fame of your wars, not the armed power of
your guard, nor the presence nearby of armed ranks unshakeable in
their strength could protect you from the base hand of one of
them and his bloody steel.   Not so did the mighty care of the
eternal father for Elizabeth fail; though she was beset by a
thousand snares and tricks she never fell from trust, but quickly
surveyed the swimming towers of the Spaniards, and conquered the
seas finally by virtue of her pious prayers and the powerful arm-
our of heaven: and so, lest her hurried fleet might fail, the
heavens, the seas, and the winged troops of the air kept fighting
for her.
     And now Garnet, in charge of Jesuitical affairs (but only
for the English), secretly gives his judgement on those on this
side of the sea who are about to go abroad wherever it be. (Bel-
gium submits to the holy voice of Cresswell, Spain to that of
Baldwin.) With increasing years, that trickster has become ever
more ready for deceit; he knows things secret and things public,
and with his feigned piety he has learnt to make sport of youth
as well as of the demented souls of old men and women.   He lives
in the deserted countryside far from the city, and a beautiful
woman of noble line ministers to the old man in her plentiful
home, nor are their lacking to the man consolations for his fear-

Tecta Catisbaeus petit haec, quibus haud alienus
Excipitur, multumque patri praefatus honorem
Consilio arcano priuatam supplicat aurem:
Huic facile auriculas vulpes concedit vtrasque,
Testibus et procul amotis compellat amanter:
Fare age, mi fili, secure quicquid acerbi,
Ambiguiue animo nunc fluctuat, en tibi fido
Pectore concilium do, solamenque paternum.
Ille pius statim tepide rogat, anne liceret
360   Sic punire malos, cadat vt bonus vnus et alter,
Quos fatum immeritos scelerato sparsit aceruo.
Quid in hoc praesul ait, si publica commoda poscunt
Et licet, et jubeo: datur vrbs obsessa, moretur
Excidium ne manu nostra positum, atque paratum,
Si duo nostrorum, tresue, intra moenia soli
Permaneant? quos hostili subducere cladi
Cum non concessum est, pereant fas, vtile multis
[Quod sit vt] impediat [tenuis] jactura pusillum,
Ridiculumque foret, priuatis publica praesint.
370   Hoc sibi concesso, quo nil optatius, audax
Iam scelus omne Catisbaeus concredere sanctis
Auribus haud dubitat, neuter tamen ore rubescit;
Qualis (proh pietas) vita est haec, [quamque pudenda]
Relligiosorum, qui coelum et tartara miscent?
Si sibi conducit facinus justum est licet ipsum
Horreret Siculus genio cogente Tyrannus.
Perdere sed patriam properanti soluere fraena,
Pro qua nemo mori metuit bonus atque fidelis,
Quin magis admotis suspensum impellere flammis,
380   Consilijsque iuuare, hoc sancti? praesidis hoc est?
Insidiatori porro, socijsque fit author
Fingendi varios sensus, vt tuta loquantur,
Atque reseruata totum confundere parte
Praecipit arte noua: veniam dat talibus, etsi
Summa salus animae premitur pretiumque futurae
Aeternae vitae: his arreptis proditor armis
Et confirmata jam pejor mente recedit.
      Fama sub haec Britonum, Fauco comitante, susurrat
Applicuisse oris Vinterum, protinus omnes
390   Anguineo retinet quos coniuratio nexu
Accelerant, et laudato cum milite laetum
Excipiunt socium sceleris, fatique latentis.
Ille fidelem animum, studiumque extollit Oeni,
Nullam in legato spem, paci se dare totos
Hesperios, rebusque suis: extrema necesse

ful life.   Catesby finds this dwelling, in which no stranger is
received, and after paying much court to the Jesuit father, pri-
vately had a word in his ear about the secret plan.   To him the
fox easily yielded both his little ears and, with witnesses far
removed, addressed him lovingly:
    "Come now, my son; speak with confidence whatever bitter or
doubtful thought is now revolving through your mind. Behold, with
trusty heart I offer you counsel and fatherly comfort."
    Straightway Catesby piously asked (without undue feeling)
whether it might be permissible to punish evil men with the
result that one or more good men might also come to grief, whom
fate has scattered undeserved in the wicked pile.
    "But if in such an instance," the leader says, "the public
good demands, it is permissible and I sanction it.   Let us take
the case of a city under seige: may its destruction, proposed
and prepared by our own hand, be delayed, if two or three of ours
remain within its walls?   When there has been no concession to
remove them from the disaster that is to engulf the enemy, it is
right that they should perish.   It would be weak and absurd to
allow a small loss to hinder what is in the interests of the
majority: public good overrides private interest."
    When this had been conceded to him - than which nothing was
more to his wishes - Catesby,   now bold, does not hesitate to
entrust the whole crime to those holy ears; neither of them, how-
ever, so much as blushed. What kind of life is this (for piety's
sake)?   And how shameful in men of religion who confound heaven
and hell.   If he put out the contract for a crime for himself,
even though it is justified, the Sicilian Tyrant would recoil at
the prick of conscience.   But to loosen the restraints on one
bent on destroying his country, on behalf of which no man good
and loyal fears to die, nay, to push one who is hesitant even
further to the approaching conflagration, and to help with coun-
sel, is this the office of a holy man, this the office of a pro-
tector?   Furthermore, for the conspirator and his associates he
becomes the author of various double meanings which he invents so
that they can speak safely in code, and with fresh craft he
advises Catesby to make the whole affair difficult to comprehend,
by witholding part of the plan.   He offers forgiveness for such
men, even if the ultimate salvation of the soul and the reward of
eternal life is hazarded.   Seizing this protective armour, the
traitor goes back, now more confirmed in his evil intent.   A rum-
our just before this whispered that Winter, in the company of
Fawkes, had landed on British shores.   Directly, all whom the
conspiracy held fast in its snake-like grip make haste,   and
receive this comrade in crime and in their hidden fate, together
with his much praised soldier. Winter praises the loyal spirit
and enthusiasm of Owen; there is no hope in the envoy, the whole
of Hesperia is giving itself up to peace and its own affairs;

Esse vel inuitis tentanda, moram esse timendam
Magnis consilijs, inimicaque frigora flammis.
Ergo Catisbaeus, non me praesaga fefellit
Mens, ait, externis plus aequo credimus, illud
400 Quod prope, quod nostrum est frigescit; ducimur vmbris
Non minus exangues; sed jam nouus excitet ardor
Languentes, pensetque moras; res clarius ipsa
Nunc loquitur, summi postquam sententia patris
Hanc pia Garneti justam pronunciat, eccum
Me testem, Orac'lum quo consultore receptum est.
Tanto laeti omnes authore impensius ardent
In facinus, coepti major fiducia surgit.
       Faucus in hunc numerum venit, Vritique minorem
Adiungunt fratrem, iuratos attamen ambos,
410 Et sacramento suscepta silentia firmant.
Accingunt operi se, tectos nocte ligones,
Rutraque transportant taciti per limina caeca,
Lignea defossis et sustentacula muris.
Pulueris igniuomi flammam, strepitumque prementis
Momen in horrendum multa vi dolia replent,
Dein sibi prospiciunt vino dapibusque sepultis,
Ingressis nec enim retro est via, ne nota crebri,
Concursusque noui suspectos reddat, ad vsus
Quae faciunt Faucus parat ipse ignotus, et alter
420 Nomine jam longe mutata sorte minister
Creditur esse tuus Perci, simulatque peritus.
Impiger at nihilo minus his Acheronticus addit
Lucifugos clausis comites, qui nocte dieque
Nunquam desistant scelerum monuisse nouorum,
Occulta lue pestiferi, immunesque figurae.
Depositis tandem generosis ensibus, armos
Expediunt, aptant manibus ruralia tela,
Fossorumque alias despecto munere laeti
Funguntur, fluit incomptis de crinibus imber.
430 Inter opus vario casus sermone futuros
Exagitant, princeps, vt si conuentibus absit
Vnde capi possit; vel dux, si perditur ille;
Regia seu virgo; procerum quibus (vtile si sit)
Parcendum, illorumque citi sub fulminis ictum
Cui summa Imperij tradant; dein extera pensant
Auxilia, Hispanos nimium tardare, timenda
Agmina Gallorum temeraria, Lutheranis
Si Bataua accedat sociali foedere classis.
Talia nequicquam sermone et mente volutant,
440 Spemque metumque interpositi sibi somnia fingunt.

even if they are unwilling it is necessary that extreme measures
be tried - hesitation is to be feared in such mighty plans and
chill delay is the enemy of fiery enterprise.   Therefore Catesby
says:
    "The foreboding in my thoughts did not deceive me. We are
putting more trust than is reasonable in external help.   What is
at hand of our own devising grows cold; by phantoms we are led
astray - and are no less bloodless ourselves. But now a new ard-
our rouses our drooping spirits and compensates for delay.   The
situation itself now speaks more clearly, after the holy word of
our father Garnet declares this affair to be just.   Behold, as I
am your witness, the oracle received by the supplicant."
    Rejoicing in such great authority they are all more eagerly
bent on crime, and greater confidence rises in their undertaking.
    Into their number comes Fawkes, and they add the younger
brother of Wright, but only after both had sworn, and a silent
taking of the sacrament confirms them. They equip themselves for
the task, and under the cover of night they silently transport
through the dark streets mattocks and spades, wood for the
trenches and props for the walls. For the moment of the terrible
conflagration they fill up large jars with the mighty power of
the fiery dust that conceals within itself flame and thunder.
Then they take provision for themselves, burying food and wine.
Nor is there the same way out for those who have entered the
place, in case it became known by frequent use, and the coming
and going makes them suspected of something novel.   Fawkes him-
self prepares what they do for readiness, himself unknown, and as
another by name, since his fortune has long been changed, is now
believed to be a servant of yours, Percy, and skillfully main-
tains the disguise.   But no less energetic, the lord of Acheron
adds companionable spirits that hate the light to those enclosed
underground, who night and ·day never cease to advise of new
crimes, pests that spread their plague unseen with form immune
from harm.   At length with their noble swords laid aside, they
set their shoulders ready, fit country weapons to their hands and
happily perform the office of diggers that otherwise they
despise. The sweat pours down from their dishevelled hair. Dur-
ing their task in various talk they raise the spectre of happen-
ings to come; how the king can be captured if absent from the
sitting, or who is to be their leader if he is destroyed, whether
it is the maiden princess; which of the lords should be spared
(if there is any profit in it); to which one of them just before
the lightning stroke they should hand over supreme command. Then
they ponder carefully foreign aid; that the Spaniards are too
slow, the troops of the French to be feared for their rashness;
whether the Dutch fleet might come to the Lutherans under a
treaty alliance.   They vainly turn over such things in their
thoughts and conversation; poised between hope and fear, they
invent for themselves the stuff of dreams.

          Interea sanctae tumulos inuisit Elizae
     Relligio pro more suo coelestis, et expers
     Terrenae molis, simulatos marmore vultus,
     Et decus antiquum reginae inspectat amatae,
     Reginae cuius diuino pectore sedit
     Insignis pietas olim, virtusque virilis.
     Artibus ergo domi pacis clarissima facta est,
     Bellorum et fama celebrata, quod extera late
     Vis sensit, proprio sed castigata flagello.
450 Imperio terraeque potens, tumidique profundi
     Regnis auxilio socijs fuit, vnde triumphis
     Claruit externis, ipsi mirabilis hosti,
     Innuba cum foret, et tantis sic [vna praeesset]
     Foemina sola viris, nusquam vt victoria pugnae
     Desereret dominos ipsa dominante Britannos.
     Ritus sacrorum reuocat veneranda vetustos,
     Pura mente Deum recolens, et simplice cultu,
     Per templa explosis nugis, fucoque latino.
     Hinc natae insidiae, bella hinc exorta, sed vnus
460 Romanis sanctis nihil aduertentibus, illam
     Texit amore suo Deus, eripuitque periclis.
     Illius vmbram obtuta, memorque notabilis aeui
     Nomen Elizaeum quod in omnia saecula sanxit,
     Viuida Relligio fundit solemnia verba.
     Non equidem regina pari tua dulcis imago
     Maiestate refert te, qualem vidimus olim
     Ingenti pompa populo spectante senatum
     Cum peteres, seu legatis cum doctior illis
     Iisdem mox responsa dares constantia linguis.
470 Sed vere effigians magis, et viuacior omni
     Marmore fama tibi monumenta perennia condet,
     Qualia custodi seruata Britannia debet.
     Hic tibi pos'ta tamen foeliciter ossa quiescant,
     Magni quae tumulo genitoris funditus olim
     Eruere vt sacris fierent ludibria flammis,
     Ingens sperabat furor, id nisi fata vetassent.
     Haec noua dicentem subit indignatio, flexis
     Propterea genibus, duplicique ad sidera verso
     Lumine trinum vno numen sic ore precata est.
480 Despice de coelo Rex o supreme, paterque
     Vere sanctorum, tenebras et viscera terrae
     Qui pernici acie penetras, motusque animorum,
     Abstrusos solus cernis, miserere tuorum,
     Fac torpere malis neruos, consultaque eorum
     Destrue, nec regem (qui sceptra potitur Elizae

Meanwhile the heavenly Religion makes her customary visit to the tomb of the divine Elizabeth, and, shedding the weight of her earthly form, looks upon the countenance feigned in marble and the ancient splendour of the beloved queen, in whose divine heart once lodged extraordinary piety and courage worthy of a man. Accordingly she became most famed in the arts of peace at home, and celebrated in fame for wars which foreign powers felt far and wide, duly but justly chastised by her whip. Powerful in her dominion on land, she brought aid on the swelling deep to allied kingdoms, whence she was famous for foreign triumphs, causing wonder to the enemy himself since she was unmarried, and thus a single woman so commanded such multitudes of men that victory in battle never deserted the ruling Britons as long as she governed them. The venerable queen restored the rites of the sacraments to their ancient form, worshipping the Lord with a pure heart and with simple ceremony, with all the nonsense and Latin adulteration dispensed with throughout our places of worship. Hence plots were hatched, hence wars broke out, but, while the Roman saints took no notice, the One God protected her with his love and saved her from all perils. Gazing upon her shadow likeness, and mindful of the famous age which has made the name of Elizabeth sacred for all generations, the living Religion poured forth her solemn words:

"Your fair image, O queen, does not indeed render you in majesty equal to that which once we saw when you made your way to Parliament with a great procession of people gazing on, or when with greater learning you instantly gave resolute replies in their own tongues to those ambassadors. But in truth your fame better figures you and, with more life than any marble, will establish eternal monuments for you such as Britain in her safety owes her protectress. Nevertheless may your bones placed here rest happily in peace, which once an insane passion hoped completely to dig up from your father's tomb so that they might become a sport for flames - this would have come to pass if the fates had not forbidden."

Indignation comes upon her as she speaks of these recent events, and on that account kneeling with both eyes turned to the stars she prays to the Godhead, three in one.

"Look down from heaven, O King most high, and true father of the holy, who with swift piercing gaze looks into the darkness and the innermost parts of the earth, and alone discerns the hidden motions of souls, pity your people, cause the sinews of the wicked to go slack, destroy their plans, and do not desert the King (who took possession of the sceptre from Elizabeth and car-

E

Magnificeque gerit) te pure, animoque colentem
Desere, ceu ferrum intentat Romana tyrannis,
Degeneremue dolum, ceu gentem euertere totam
Cogitat occulta, non sperataque ruina.
490   Nam magis atque magis numero turba improba crescit,
Iamque aliquid minitatur, at o tu maxime custos
Sis vigil vsque precor, Britonumque tuere salutem;
Nec grex ille tui turgens sub nomine nati
Cunctorum exuperans longe malefacta suorum
Pestifer in vitas valeat, tumulosue bonorum;
Haec pia vaticinans lachrimis remoratur abortis.
Ecce repentinus demissa in lumina fulgor
Claros insinuat radios, caput ergo caducum
Paulatim releuans ardentem conspicit alis
500   Sidereis juuenem, specie qui pulchrior omni
Emicat humanus quam visus percipit, aut mens:
Attonitaeque fauens jucunde talia fatur;
Ne tu nunc vltra charum sanctissima virgo
Perge malis Anglorum animum cruciare timendis,
Assiduae valuere preces, pater optimus aurem
Reclusit, casti vincit constantia voti.
De summo elapsum me conditor orbis Olympo
Dat vigilem fatis regni, regisque Britanni;
Dixerat, et [leuiter tenues] se fudit in auras.
510   Illa, die veluti sacro pulsa organa templis
Cum resonant cantante choro, de pectore tollit
Ingenti coeleste melos, latera alta sacelli
Pressa gemunt, magna monumentaque saxea voce:
Omnia donantis dum laudes enthea cantat,
Et nullis aequanda sonis opera omnipotentis.
Te templis recinam, te celsis montibus inquit
Alme pater, media vrbe, inter deserta ferarum,
Nec loca sunt tam sola quibus non inclita splendent
Signa potestatis vestrae, vel pignus amoris.
520   Grataque tum longa serie primo orbis ab ortu
Admiranda dei memori de pectore promit.
Dum vetera enumerat, crescunt noua facta, nec vnquam
Dormiscit bonitas summi, aeternique parentis.
Caeca etenim motu prudentia ducta superno,
Vicini quasi praeuideat iam fata diei,
Prorogat indictum noua per consulta senatum.
Hinc atrum turbatur opus, mediumque relinquunt
Diri fossores, sed mens eadem ipsa nocendi
Indefessa manet, praeterlapsisque diebus
530   In fossas redeunt alacres, muroque minantur.

ries it magnificently,   the King who worships you   in purity and
with all his heart)   just as Roman tyranny threatens the sword or
a base plot,   just as it contemplates subverting the whole nation
in unseen and   unexpected ruin.   For the   wicked rabble increases
more and more,   and now begins to threaten some menace,   but you,
most mighty guardian, be watchful,   I ever pray,   and look to the
safety of the Britons.   Neither let that pestilential band,
swelling in number in the name of your son and far outdoing the
crimes of all their kind,   prevail against the lives or the tombs
of the good."

With this pious utterance of foreboding, she lingers in use-
less tears.   Behold, a sudden   lightning flash darted its clear
rays into her downcast eyes,   and so lifting her fallen head lit-
tle by little she catches sight of a youth glowing with starry
wings who in his whole appearance shone forth with more beauty
than sight and mind perceive.   Showing favour to her in her
amazement, he spoke sweetly as follows:

"Do not (holiest of maidens) now continue further to torture
your precious soul in fear of the wicked among the English.   Con-
stant prayer has proved its power.   Our Father most good has
opened his ear.   The steadfastness of pure prayer prevails.   The
founder of the world grants that I come down from highest heaven
to watch over the fate of the kingdom and of the British King."

He had spoken, and lightly dissolved into thin air.   Just as
the organ is struck up on a sacred day in churches,   when it
resounds to the singing choir, so she raises from her mighty
heart a heavenly song; the monumental stone and the high walls of
the chapel make moan,   struck with the mighty voice,   as she,
divinely inspired, sings the praises of the giver of all things,
and the works of him who is all powerful that cannot be matched
in sound.

"Let me sing of you again in the churches" (she says) "in
the highest mountains,   benificent Father, in the midst of the
city and among the deserted places of the wild beasts; nor are
there places so forsaken in which the illustrious signs of your
power and the pledge of your love do not shine forth."

And then she pours forth from her ever mindful heart all the
wonders of God's grace in long succession from the first rising
of the earth. While she numbers those of old, new deeds become
visible, nor does the goodness of the eternal father in the high-
est ever incline to sleep.   For unconscious foresight, guided by
a motion from above, as if it already could foresee the fates of
the next day,   deferred the appointed council by fresh decrees.
Hence the dark work was thrown into confusion,   and the fearful
diggers abandon their work unfinished.   But there remains the
same indefatigable disposition to ill, and after a lapse of days
they eagerly return to their tunnels,   and threaten the wall.

Praesagos ignes silici dum cuspide stringunt
Vani fatidici, subito magnoque fragore
Terrentur, sed res placet explorata, relictam
Inueniunt siquidem cameram quae proxima muro est
Illam conducunt, illuc vim sulphuris omnem
Traijciunt, miscent cum puluere ferramenta,
Et super impositis lignis, carboneque multo,
Aggestisque cadis zithi cellaria fingunt.
Exigitur nullis opus obseruantibus, omnis
540 Tuta loco spes est, studijs fatalibus apto.
Iamque tremendi ictus momentum triste propinquat,
Et votis spacium breue tantum immanibus obstat.
Cum celebris noua conuentus suspensio plures
Delati in lunas (monitu illam rege jubente
Non sine diuino) securos opprimit, et spes
Illusas veluti suauissima somnia grandi
Turbinis abrumpit stridore, huc ergo redacti
Consilijs habitis priuatos quisque recessus
Diuisi repetunt [suspectos se fore iunctos]
550 Credebant siquidem, et solis opus esse tenebris.
Sic vbi munita conclusi naue feruntur
Ausis terribiles magis ingenioque nociuo
Quam tumidi numero piratae, [per vada noctu]
[Oppidulum] nulla pensata fraude quietum
Oppressuri, Euris aduersis saepe repulsi
Spe praedae toties redeunt, totiesque recedunt
Sublatis ventis, metuentes denique lucis
Indicium sese subducunt, et procul abdunt,
Donec tempestas spolijs matura recurrit:
560 Haud secus horribiles, obfirmatique latrones
Funeribus nostris inhiant, tecteque repressis
Prospiciunt flammis, sitiunt praecordia caedem.
Fauci praecipua est celandi primaque cura,
Ne personatum prodat mora longa, proinde.
Ad Belgas missus redit vt committat Oeno
Pulueris arcanum, et Stanlaeum in crimina jungat
Magnas qui virtutis opes dare transfuga turpi
Non metuit sceleri, et dominis sua jura superbis,
Sic vt jam facti nil poenituisse juuabit.
570 Ad mare promissis hos auxiliaribus armis
Admonet expectent vt prima incendia, turbis
Succedantque nouis, ipsisque authoribus adsint
Mature, facilem dum se victoria praebet.
Garneti pariter Baldino cognita signo
Scripta dat, ambo patres cum sint, et munere fratres.

While these vain prophets draw their divining fires from the
pointed flint, they are terrified by a sudden and mighty crash,
but on investigation the matter pleases, since they discover a
vault which is very near the wall. They rent it, transfer the
whole quantity of their sulphur there, put their iron implements
in with the powder, place their wood on top, and with much char-
coal and heaped up beer barrels they fashion their cellars. The
work is carried out unobserved, all their hope is safe in a place
well fitted for deadly schemes. And now the sombre moment for
the fearful blow approaches, and only a brief interval stands in
the way of the completion of their monstrous designs, when a new
suspension of Parliament, now delayed for many months (ordered by
the king not without divine prompting) dashed their security and
their illusory hopes like the sweetest dreams broken in upon by
the mighty whirring of a stormy wind. Accordingly, after holding
council, they were driven to the expedient of splitting up, each
man making for his private retreat, since they believed that
together they would be suspected, and there was especial need for
the cover of darkness. As when pirates on the sea at night in a
well-armed ship, (more to be feared for their reckless daring and
their natural inclination to ill than because they boast of num-
bers) who are bent on the destruction of a peaceful little town
that has no suspicion of treachery, are often driven back in the
teeth of the Easterlies, so often they return in hope of booty
and as often retire before the rising winds, and then fearing the
disclosure of day they steal away and hide far off until a time
ripe for spoil returns: scarcely otherwise these hateful and
obstinate brigands longingly anticipate our death, and look for-
ward to the fire secretly held in check, while their hearts
thirst for slaughter. The prime and overriding concern of Fawkes
is for concealment in case the long delay should bring their pre-
tence to light. He is sent back to Belgium to disclose the
secret of the powder plot to Owen, and to recruit Stanley to the
crime, who, as a deserter, does not fear to commit the copious
resources of his courage to the wicked outrage, and so give his
judgements to his proud masters that it will not be in their
interest to have washed their hands of the deed. He warns Stan-
ley to wait for the initial conflagration with the auxiliary
forces which he has promised by sea, to follow after with fresh
numbers and to be present with the instigators of the plot, while
victory still offers itself easily. He gives him letters from
Garnet, known equally to Baldwin by their seal, since both are
fathers of the church and brothers in office. And now with equal

Iamque pari in rabiem Romanam pectore surgunt,
In scelus, et caedem immensam, Albionumque ruinam.
Nuntius ex Anglis itidem praemittitur oris
Summo Pontifici, sancti qui perferat huius
580   Famam operis, decoris pleni, meritique beati.
Praefixoque die Ausoniae pietatis alumni
Quotquot erant, terra late licet, aequore et amplo
Partiti, prece communi, junctisque querelis
Numina sollicitant sua; libertatis auitae
Ex his festinum reditum conatibus orant,
Ignotis tamen et lachrymarum gurgite. sparsim
Vota immunda lauant, sed quae non eluet imus
Oceanus fluuijs adiutus, et imbribus altis.
Fama duos perhibet latos, multumque profundos
590   Esse lacus, lachrymis miserorum vtrosque dicatos.
Puris conspiciendus aquis stat limphidus vnus,
Floribus ad ripas [toto vernantibus anno,]
Et (si fas vti) generosis viribus herbis:
Sidereus vigil hinc abigit mergosque, strigesque,
Omnigenasque feras, namque huc lachrymata piorum
Flumina lecta ferunt superi, aligerique ministri,
Et caste seruant chari monumenta doloris.
Gurgite coenosus sed cernitur alter opaco,
Serpentum genitor, tollens animalcula visu
600   Horrida, mortiferis, varijsque referta venenis:
At foris exudat monachorum aconita cucullos,
Solanumque furens, risu et quod sternit amaro
Sardiniae laethum, Colchorum dulceque virus.
Infestas lachrymas simul exprimit improba turba
Huc raptas cogunt liuentis Alastoris vmbrae,
Conduntque vt testes olim maeroris iniqui.
Atque ibidem noua nunc Stygius fleta aequora visens
Tantis optantum studijs horrenda triumphat.
Sacrifici interea rem maturare laborant,
610   Et coniurati rata nunc ad foedera plures
Alliciunt, Vinterum annis opibusque priorem
Fratre infoelici; Grantam, vnanimumque Rucodem,
Tressainumque agris et auita gente superbum,
Et clarum Digbaeum equitem, Caiumque, Batumque,
Quem modo Tesmundus nutantem, animoque cruentum
Horrentem facinus firmauerat; hos, aliosque
Illaqueant, et equos belloque occulta futuro
Arma parant, loca disponunt, et tempora rebus;
Omnia festinant, nam laetus, et integer illis
620   Gaudet adhuc properare dies, optatus et instat.

enthusiasm they are drawn into the Roman madness, into the crime, the mighty carnage and the ruin of Albion.   Likewise an envoy is sent in advance from English shores to the supreme Pontiff to carry news of this holy work that is full of glory and heaven-blessed merit.   On a pre-arranged day the nurslings of Italian piety, all those who had been distributed far and wide over land and boundless sea, solicit their divinities with common prayer and a united sense of grievance; they pray for the swift return of their ancient freedom as a result of these endeavours, excused in a wash of tears. Here and there they wash their unclean desires, but the deepest ocean aided by rivers and rain water from above will not wash them clean.

Fame tells of two broad and extremely deep lakes, both devoted to the tears of the wretched. One stands clear and lucid, its water pure, with spring flowers blooming on its banks all the year round, and (if use of them were proper) herbs of benificent power. From here a starry sentinel keeps away screech owls and divers, and every kind of wild beast; for hither the winged ministers of heaven bring the waters they have collected from the weeping of the faithful, and they chastely guard the memorials of their precious pain. But the other is seen to be muddy with murky waters, a breeding ground of snakes, raising to the sight small creatures that cause a shudder, replete with a variety of deadly poisons. But from its banks it exudes aconite, monks hood, nightshade that maddens, and from Sardinia laethum that convulses with bitter laughter, and the sweet venom of the Colchians. As soon as the impudent multitude shed their hateful tears, spirits of the envious Avenger snatch them, collect them here, and store them as witnesses of once wicked grief. And now seeing fresh oceans of tears there, the Stygian triumphs in the inordinate enthusiasm of those who desire abominable deeds.

Meanwhile the sacrificers work hard to bring the matter to a head. And the conspirators now entice more to the established compact; Winter, greater than his ill-starred brother in years and wealth, Grant, of one mind with Rookwood, Tresham proud in lands and ancestral lineage, Digby the illustrious knight, Keyes and Bates whom, though wavering and recoiling within from the bloody crime, Tesimond had just made sure; these and others they ensnare. They make ready their horses and hidden arms for the war to come, and make their dispositions of place and time for the event. They hurry on with everything, for the happy and per-fect day still delights to hasten for them, and, much longed for,

Externas quoque spes rediens confirmat abunde
Faucus, et incendit mercata laude furentes.
Iamque cateruatim sopitam suscitat vrbem
Rhedarumque, equitumque fragor, toto vndique regno
Confluit vt populus solenni more vocatus.
Spectandam plebi ad pompam subsellia prostant
Consuetis erecta locis, magnoque propinquas
Conducunt pretio meliori ex sorte fenestras.
Regem, reginamqe, et te charissime princeps
630 Visendi fit tantus amor, dum fata sinebant,
Crescentemque in regna ducem (si forte tenellus
Accedat numero) nunc cernere magna lubido est.
Templorum decus, atque fori, venerandaque regni
Canities grauitate sua spectabilis ipsa est:
Insignes et equis phaleratis agmine longo
Coccineisque togis proceres incedere pulchrum.
Tanta sed haec, nisi prospiciat deus vltima nostris
Gloria resplendens post secula multa futura est.
Pernicies suprema latet, quam praecipit ales
640 Aethereus, jussuque dei, cui sedulus vni
Paret, mortales facili molimine vultus
Induit, at quales ignota in plebe videre est,
Seruilis facies, habitusque oblonga statura;
Talis litterulas signatas vespere defert
Montegli famulo, domino mox reddat vt illas,
Dein se subduxit, leuibusque immiscuit auris.
Perlegit has juuenis veteri qui stemmate clarus
Cum sibi nescio quid magni promittere visae,
Nec tamen apparens author, vel nuntius illis,
650 Caecilium festinus adit, cui tradita regni
Cura, dat inque manus priuatas nobile scriptum,
Et procerem vt decet exceptus cum laude recedit.
Conuocat eximios aliquot sibi, munera quorum
In commune eadem sunt, et clam prouidus ille
Discutit obscurae quae sit sententia chartae:
Magnanimusque licet contemnere talia sueuit,
Nunc haeret, sensus turbata mente volutans
Ambiguos, sed nequiciquam Deus abnegat illis
Hunc tantum, soli quem sceptro assignat honorem.
660 Ergo fatigati studio (ceu Delphica quondam
Templa) adeunt thalamos maiori numine regis
Imbuti, turgens tribuit quam Graecia Phoebo.
Illius experto implorant ab acumine, scripto
Oblato auxilium, lucemque huic nube remota.
Ponderat acceptam schedulam rex, terque quaterque

presses near.   On his return Fawkes greatly strengthens their
hope of foreign aid,   and fires their passions with mercenary
praise.   And now the noise of the carriages and their cavalry in
troops arouses the city from its sleep, from the whole kingdom on
all sides they pour together like a people in solemn fashion sum-
moned.   Seats are put out for the people to see the procession,
set up in their customary places, and nearby windows are hired
out at great price by their lucky owners. So great is the love of
seeing the King, the Queen, and you, most precious prince, while
the fates allowed;   and now there is a great desire to see the
Duke growing to his royal part (if there were any chance of his
tender person being added to their number). The splendour of the
churches and of the square, and the awesome antiquity of the mon-
archy in its grave majesty, is spectacle in itself.   Also out-
standing, processing in a long column on caparisoned horses with
their scarlet robes, are the lords, a beautiful sight.   But this
great glory, resplendent for many generations to come, is the
last of its kind for our people,   should God not exercise his
foresight.   The supreme calamity lurks unseen, which the winged
agent of heaven perceives, and on the order of God, whom alone he
zealously obeys, puts on a mortal face with easy effort, but one
such as might be seen in any anonymous crowd, a servant's face,
with clothing rather long in size.   As such at night he brings
down sealed letters to the servant of Monteagle, so that he might
soon take them to his master.   Then he withdraws and vanishes
into thin air.   These the youth illustrious in his lineage reads
through, since they seem to promise something of importance to
him.   However no author is apparent and no envoy either.   He
quickly goes to Cecil to whom has been handed over the care of
the realm, and puts the celebrated document into his hands. And,
as befits a lord, he withdraws covered in praise.   Cecil summons
a number of distinguished men who hold office in the Council, and
on the watch for some disaster, he discusses the meaning of the
obscure manuscript.   Though his noble spirit was accustomed to
despise such things, he now pays close attention, turning over
the doubtful meaning in his anxious mind, but in vain; God keeps
it from all except from him to whom alone he assigns the honour
of the sceptre. And so, wearied with their study, they go (as to
the Delphic temple) to the chambers of the king who is inspired
by a greater power than proud Greece attributed to Phoebus.
Handing over the letter, they seek the help of his well-tried
genius in removing the obscurity and shedding light upon the mat-
ter.   The king ponders the small paper that he has been given,

Percurrens oculique acie mentisque beatae.
[Consulit haec procer abstineat] se charta Senatu
Primo sole, diem fore nam coeuntibus illum
Infaustum, quos non sensuros opprimet ictus
670   Terribilis, turbis haud apparentibus vllis.
Ac veluti recta puluis ratione paratus
Flammifer admotos facile mox sentiet ignes,
Pulueream haud aliter (trutinatis ordine verbis)
Terribili exposito fraudem rex concipit ictu;
Omnes cui merito applaudunt, proin acrius illuc
Tenditur, vt loca sint caute [scrutanda] senatus,
Quo dolus aut pateat, lateat vel causa timoris.
Ast operae Cneuetus eques bene cognitus ipsi
Praeficitur, color amissas est quaerere furto
680   Reginae vestes, surrepta aulaeaque regis.

casting over it three or four times the beam of his eye and his
heaven-blessed intelligence. The letter advises the lord to keep
himself away from the assembly chamber next morning, for that day
will be inauspicious for the makers of assemblies upon whom will
come unsuspecting a terrible blow, though the upheaval is without
apparent sign.   And just as explosive powder properly primed is
straightway readily sensitive to the flame that is put to it,
just so having duly weighed these words, the king conceived the
gunpowder plot in a terrible lightning flash.   All rightly
applaud him, then they eagerly make their way thither, with the
intention that the whole area around the chamber be carefully
searched, so that the plot might be revealed, or the cause of
their fear be allayed.   But Knyvett, a well known knight, is put
in charge of the operation itself,   on the pretext of secretly
investigating the lost clothes of the queen and the stolen tapes-
tries of the king.

Liber 2

Argumentum

Faucus vt opportune opera fatoque prehensus
Cneueti scelus expandit, cameramque secundus
Persequitur liber; excusso noua gaudia somno
Rex placide admittit; tota quae, luce renata,
Vrbe calent: studio capiendae fingit Elizae
Venatum multis Digbaeus cinctus amicis.
Vindictam statuit populo acclamante senatus:
Ignati vmbra animos impellit ad arma rebelles.
Conjuratorum foedantur puluere vultus,
10 Pugnae mox caesi qui sunt, captiue sub vmbra.

   His vix digestis premit oras Oceani sol,
Mane cui ignaro spectacula quanta parantur,
Quam taciti sceleris plena, et maeroris acerbi?
Sed neque prodigiosi ignes, nec turbinis atri
Insolitus fragor ardentes terrebat equorum
Praecipitantum animos, non fluxum, aut pensile monstrum
Nox tenebris contenta suis, et luna vetustis
Sideribus, nec spectra solo dant, nec noua coelo
Signa, sed innocue per amica silentia vadunt.
20 Eduntur clausis suspiria nulla sepulchris
Non audita strigum vox, non ignoti vlulatus,
Tympana nulla tremunt, nec murmura maesta tubarum.
Numinis offensi nondum praenunciat iram,
Occultiue metum portenti inamabile quidquam.
   Tempus erat penitus victis mortalia curis
Alta inspiratos traherent cum pectora somnos,
Ante fores Faucus (vacua cui Percius aede
Omnia permisit) stat solus, et vltimus ausi
Tanti, parque actor; sed enim quid mentis habere
30 Impius, aut animi potuit? fastigia templi

Book Two

The Argument

The Second Book continues by describing how Fawkes, caught in the nick of time by the operation of Knyvett and by fate, opens up the room and lays bare the crime. Shaking off sleep, the king calmly allows fresh rejoicing, which, when day returns, grows warm throughout the whole city. In eagerness to capture Elizabeth, Digby, surrounded by many friends, invents a hunting expedition. The council at the people's clamouring decides on vengeance. The ghost of Ignatius drives the rebel spirits to arms. The faces of the conspirators are scorched by gunpowder, and they are either slain at once, or consigned to dark captivity.

Scarcely had these arrangements been made, when the sun presses hard upon the bounds of the ocean in the morning. Can it not know how great are the spectacles prepared for it, how full of hidden wickedness and bitter grief? But there were no ominous fires, and no unusual stirring of a dark storm wind to terrify the impassioned spirits of the bolting horses, nor did the Night at peace with its own shadows, or the Moon with its stars of old, afford any flux of water or prodigious shooting star; they continue indifferently in benign silence and do not give any apparitions on the ground or new signs in the sky. No sighs issue from closed tombs, no cry of the screech owl is heard, no unaccountable wailings, no tremor of drumbeats, nor mournful sound of trumpets. And no shuddering fear of any hidden portent points in advance to the anger of an offended godhead. It was the time when the hearts of men with their cares completely vanquished draw in the sleep that is breathed down from on high. Before his doors Fawkes (to whom Percy had allowed the freedom of his house) stands alone, the last actor in this reckless play, and one equal to his part. But what kind of mind or heart could he have, the

Si dubia forsan licuit pertingere luce,
Perdita seu tantum versus loca lumina sacra
Tenderet, antiquis regum veneranda sepulchris,
Omnia momento quae fundere sperat, et audet?
Sacra prophana vnum est, scelus imperterritus ardet,
Quicquid et ingentem poterit celebrare ruinam.
Hunc ibi Cneuetus cunctantem vt cernit (adesse
Quem vigilum stipante globo iam fata monebant)
Prendi suspectum iubet, et numquid tegat arcte
40   Quaeri, funiculos ad sola incendia natos
Et quae conducunt his instrumenta scelesti
Vestibus expromunt rimantes; nec mora captus
Denudatusque intrepido coeptum ore fatetur,
Ac veluti justo turget, coelumque merenti,
Nec nisi non facto dolet: horribilisque recluso
Fornice letiferum cumulum mirantibus addit,
Faucum istic, dudum quo festinabat, adortum
Tota cum turba succensa mole seipsum
Flammis deuouisse prius quam vincula ferret;
50   Tam miro ambiguos nectit Deus ordine casus.
Praepositis camerae custodibus, illico vinctum
Monstrum execrantes ad sacra palatia ducunt,
Vt fit ubi fidis canibus latrantibus vrsum
Concurrente trahunt multa per compita plebe;
Insomnes aula proceres quid pulueris affert
Nuncius expectant, noua qui pandente stupescunt
Cneueto, nec se retinent, quin protinus omnes
Nocte intempesta licet haec sua gaudia vati
Sceptrigero asportent, ceu visa insomnia somno.
60   Praecedit reliquos thalamorum munere custos
Excelso duce prognatus Suffolcius heros,
Quo patriae nec erat, nec regis amantior alter,
Impatiensque morae vix dum satis experrectum
Inclamat dominum; patet omnis fraus, patet ingens
Infandumque scelus; loca sunt suspecta senatus
Puluere onusta, tenet tanti custodia furti
Artificem: regum o decus, o ter maxime vates,
Te populo, populumque tibi, tria regnaque solus
Seruasti, tua nos nunquam praesagia fallunt.
70   Per te diua vxor, per te tua regia proles,
Per te jam numenque tuum nos viuimus omnes,
Spiramusque tibi debetur ciuica laurus,
Et capiti veris diademata lucida stellis.
Laetus, et vt sanctum decuit mox lumina coelo
Attollens, sacrasque manus rex feruidus infert:

impious man?   If chance had allowed him actually to reach the
depths of the sacred chamber in the half light, or if he were
only to turn his desperate eyes in the direction of these hal-
lowed places venerable with the ancient tombs of kings, all of
which he hopes to destroy in a moment, would he still be bold?
Sacred, prophane, it is one. Unperturbed he longs for the wicked
deed and whatever can make the great ruin celebrated.   When Kny-
vett caught sight of him lingering there (for fate warned that he
was there to be a guard for the compressed fireball) he ordered
him to be held on suspicion and searched to see if he was hiding
anything close to him.   Searching, they take out of his clothes
fuse wires and devices which criminals use for setting fires.
Without delay he is arrested and stripped, and he confesses the
deed in fearless tones, and takes pride in it as something justi-
fied and serving heaven, nor does he show any remorse except that
it had not been accomplished.   The terrible man opens up the
vault, discloses the deathly pile and adds the crowning wonder,
that he, when he had reached the place to which he had just been
hastening, would have sacrificed himself to the flames with the
whole crowd in a mighty conflagration before he would have
endured chains.   In such wondrous wise does God dispose of doubt-
ful events.   When they had first posted guards in the room, they
lead the unnatural man, bound there and then, to the sacred pal-
ace, pouring down curses upon him, as happens when men drag a
bear through the streets to the accompaniment of barking dogs and
a crowd of the common people.   The lords, awake in the palace,
wait for news of the plot, and when Knyvett reveals the recent
discoveries they are dumbfounded, and cannot restrain themselves
even at that unreasonable hour of the night from straightway car-
rying their rejoicing like dreams seen in sleep to the prophetic
seer who holds the sceptre. The keeper of the bedchamber, son of
a noble duke, precedes the rest - the hero Suffolk, than whom
none is more loving to his king and country, and, impatient of
delay, he calls to his master (who is scarcely fully awakened
from sleep):
    "All the treachery is made manifest, manifest is the great
unspeakable crime.   The suspected places about the council cham-
ber are laden with gunpowder. The deviser of this great plot is
held by the guard.   O glory of kings, O thrice great seer, you
have saved yourself for your people, you have saved your people
for yourself, and alone you have saved the triple kingdom; your
prophecies never fail us. Through you, your divine wife, through
you, the royal progeny, through you and your godhead we all now
live and breathe the air.   To you is owed the civic laurel, and
for your head a crown shining with true stars."
    Full of joy and as becomes a saint, straightway lifting his
eyes and his sacred hands to heaven the king gives ardent utter-
ance:

Haec tua sunt patrone Deus, tua sola fatemur
Sunt immensa opera, at multo clementia maior.
Liberiore dein sermone sopore fugato
Laetitiam celebrant hanc festam, quamque quotannis
80   Natos natorum semper renouare iuuabit.
Sic tandem tenebris exhaustis quinta Nouembris
Candida lux coelo surgit, qua faustior aeuo
Non vlla exposuit radios, nec postera promet.
Iamque exurgenti factis operisque diurnis
Vrbanae plebi, simul horum fama notescit,
Heu quantus stupor accessit? [quam viuida feruent]
Gaudia? nec capiunt euentus saepe volutos
Exiguae mentes, nec se satiare loquendo
Possunt, nec satis illa sibi fecisse putando.
90   Venatum simulat Digbaeus rure frequentem
Oblectamentum, quo nil prius, et minus ipsa
Natura nocuum, lepori detexere gressus
Sive lubet, celeres seu cursu euincere ceruos.
Longe aliud Digbaeus agit, nec vultibus aegrum
Dissimulare animum potuit, nec voce sagaces
Pro more exhilarare canes, stupet anxius, et se
Neglecto suspendit equo, sibi pondus, et illi;
Accelerans fatum, capiendaque regia virgo
Sollicitant hominem sua quem fortuna beauit.
100 Horum sed nil te metuentem, o dulcis Eliza,
Exercet pietatis amor, virtutis et artes
Augustae et quales debentur mollibus annis.
Vultu candor inest, mens candida, sideris instar
Luce micas plena semper, sine labe, vel vmbra;
Per te aditum sperare audet scelus? horrida per te
Bella ciere tubis quas dira inflabit Erinnys?
Post fratres caesos, commactatosque parentes
Solane tu regnare potes, vel praeda coacta
Sanguineum patrio capies ex hoste maritum?
110 Te dea, te leuiora manent, melioraque fata,
Grata Palatini quondam connubia nectes,
Atque triumphali duce Rhenum ardebis amore
Visere, natorum mox foelicissima mater:
Perpetuusque viae comes hinc cum conjuge fida
Ibit Haringtonus, cuius nunc [sub lare tuto]
Flos sacer inuitis praedonibus ipsa virescis,
Amborum pia cura, et delectabile pignus.
Sed reducem sua tecta senem (sic astra minantur)
Haud vnquam excipient, nec cernet patria tellus,
120 Mors iter obsidio premet, affectusque seniles.

"We acknowledge these mighty works to be yours,   O God our
protector, yours alone; but much greater even than these is your
mercy."
     Then, with all trace of sleep banished, they celebrate with
freer speech this festal joy, which it will profit our sons' sons
ever to renew year after year.   Thus at last with darkness dis-
pelled the fair light of November the fifth rises in the sky,
than which no happier day has ever put forth its rays in all
time, nor will in time to come.   And now the city people wake to
their tasks and daily round; as soon as news of the discoveries
is made known, alas how great the stupefaction that follows, how
lively is the rejoicing that rages.   And those of small under-
standing often do not grasp complex events,   and cannot satisfy
themselves in speech, nor could they be contented in their imagi-
nation alone.
     In the country Digby devises a hunt with great numbers, a
delight to which, by virtue of its very nature, nothing is
superior, or could be less harmful,   whether the pleasure be to
follow the tracks of a hare or overtake swift stags in the chase.
Far off Digby pursues another track, nor could he hide the trou-
bled spirit in his face, or inspire the keen-scented hounds with
his customary call. He is anxious and worried, and neglecting
his horse keeps himself in suspense, a burden alike to himself
and to his beast.   His hastening fate and the capture of the
royal Elizabeth worry the man whom his own lot made fortunate.
Fearing nothing of this, love of piety exercises you, O sweet
Elizabeth, and the august arts of virtue and such things as are
due to tender years.   Honesty sits in your face,   your mind is
honest, you always shine full of light like a star without blem-
ish or shadow.   Does the impious crime dare to hope for legiti-
macy through you?   Have they raised terrible wars with their
trumpets which a dread Fury will blow into around you? After the
murder of your brothers and the sacrifice of your parents, will
you be able to reign alone, or, compelled to be a spoil of war,
will you take a husband from your father's enemies who are cov-
ered in his blood?   A lighter and better fate awaits you, godd-
ess.   One day you will make a marriage alliance with Palatine,
and with a conquering general you will long with love to see the
Rhine, soon a most favoured mother of sons.   And a constant
friend from here with his faithful wife will go with you on your
way, that is Harington, under whose safe protection in spite of
the brigands' wishes you will blossom into a sacred flower, the
pious concern of them both, and a sacred pledge of delight.   But
his roof will never welcome this aged man back again (this the
stars do threaten) nor will his country see him again; death with
slow seige and old age's decay will check his journey.

F

            Musa reflecte gradum, vocat vrbs, ardensque senatus
     Vindicta, atque odio juste execrabilis ausi.
     Sanctis ergo deo votis templo ante solutis
     Assueta ingreditur pompa rex aureus aedes
     E flamma ereptas, solioque insedit auito.
     Principibusque viris in morem vtrinque locatis,
     Surgit Elismerus, sua nude jura crepantis
     Qui legis moderator erat, custosque sigilli,
     Vtque erat insigni grauitate verendus, et ore,
130 Sic prior excelsi est pro ritu muneris orsus.
            Quae mihi sunt huic apta loco meditata, reique
     Propositae, tibi soli o rex praeuisa repressit
     Res noua, res maior quam possit vocibus vllis
     Aequari, mente extensa vel tota subiri.
     Nil aeuo tale o patres proceresque priori
     Auditum, haec quoque vix credent fortasse minores;
     Vixque sui fecere fidem licet eruta vulgi
     Eminuere oculis sceleris documenta nefandi:
     Quamlibet et clare monstri caput omnia profert
140 Veris [insanus] fari maiora videtur.
     Certa nimis tamen his latuere pericula tectis,
     Pernicies aderat prope, sed propior deus; atris
     Fulminibus foetam qui nubem luce retexit
     Vni praemissa regi, vatique Jacobo.
     Illi laus igitur sit, in omneque gloria seclum;
     Huic vero vt patriae sit gratia summa parenti.
     Vnde autem scelus hoc manat si quaeritis, alma
     Fit rea relligio, pietas caedem atque rapinam
     Nempe sitit,clemens deus haec incendia poscit.
150 Authores Romae seruos habet, vltimus actor
     Molem cuius erat funestam accendere munus
     [Solus turre nimis digna custode tenetur,]
     Vrbe latent reliqui, obscuri vel rure vagantur.
     Insidijs olim hinc satis vrgebamur et armis
     Substrato nunc igne; quid expectabimus vltra?
     Spem regni et decus omne vno sufflamine (totus
     Horresco referens) [rutilas sparsisse per auras]
     Sperabant occulti hostes, nec parcere regi
     Tam placido, abstinuisse suis nec denique norunt.
160 Pulueris his ergo ruituri in fulgura tectis
     Pondera supposuere cadis ingentia plenis
     Nostram in pernitiem, mista et ferrugine multa
     Aetnaeas implent latebras quo certior ictus
     Vndique securos maiori strage feriret,
     Cum capite et sacro simul omnes perderet artus.

O muse, turn back your step.   The city and the council
ardently call for vengeance, and justly, with hatred for the
abominable attempt.   And so when sacred offerings of thanks had
been first rendered to God in church, the resplendent king with
customary ceremony enters the building snatched from the flames
and sat upon his ancestral throne.   And when the chief men in the
realm had been positioned in order on both sides, Ellesmere, who
was keeper of the seal and controller of the law (which otherwise
rattles its decrees defencelessly) arose, and as he was revered
for outstanding gravity and power of speech, so he rose first
according to the dignity of his high office.

"This new affair, foreseen by you alone, O king, has put in
the shade what I had thought appropriate for this occasion and
for the business that was put before us, being matter greater
than can be matched by any voice or wholly comprehended by even a
deep understanding.   There was nothing such in time past, O my
lords, and former leaders and perhaps our successors will
scarcely believe this when they hear it.   Ordinary people
scarcely believed it, even though proofs of the abominable crime
were clearly visible to their eyes.   However clearly anyone
reveals the principal part of the portentous event in all its
aspects, he seems to be a madman, exaggerating beyond what could
be true.   Nevertheless the dangers hidden in these halls were
only too real, destruction was near at hand; but God was nearer,
who drew back the thunderbolt-filled cloud with illumination
entrusted in advance to our one king and prophet James.   Let
praise be due to him then, and glory for all generations.   To him
truly let there be a country's thanks as to a father.   If you ask
from whence this crime spreads, religion is the culprit that
breeds crime, piety is the same and truly thirsts for plunder:
'God in his mercy demands this conflagration'.   The perpetrator
whose final task it was to set alight this funeral pile has for
his authority the servants of Rome.   He is held alone in the
tower, too worthy a prison.   The rest remain hidden in the city
or roam the countryside in obscurity.   In the past from this
quarter we were pressed by armed plots, now by fire laid beneath
our feet.   What more shall we expect?   Our hidden enemies were
hoping (I recoil in total horror as I tell it) to have scattered
through the scorching air the hope and glory of the realm in a
single explosion, and they know not to spare a king so peace-lov-
ing, or when to call a halt to their efforts.   And so they put
under these buildings heavy quantities of fuel with jars full of
ruinous powder for a lightning strike, and our destruction; with
this they mix much lead and so fill up their concealed volcano
that the blow may hit more surely with greater slaughter coming
everywhere on the unsuspecting, and that with their sacred head
it might destroy the limbs together.

Heu quibus orba suo miseranda Britannia sole
Plangeret in tenebris, luna, atque minoribus astris,
Principe sublato duce, syderijsque puellis?
Quis templis lumen praeberet? rura quis arte
170   Aspera corrigeret, pacemque imponeret armis?
Per fora quis lites sedaret iure paterno?
Quae demum insultus externos cura caueret?
Vincentis quae vis sceleris froenare furorem
Grassantem interne poterat? matrumue leuare,
Vxorum aut luctus quae tum solatia possent?
Momento clades si tantaque, tamque inopina
Contigerat media positis in pace Britannis;
Cunctis ordinibus velut vno fulmine fusis.
Sic tua, Roma, furit rabies, horrendaque proles
180   Ignati, ambiguus commisto daemone partus.
Quo, rex, vsque feres mala tot mitissime multa?
Infoelix sibi quem statuet patientia finem?
Iam placabilitas nocet, impunitaque crescet
Nequitia in seram tandem nutrita ruinam.
Non est quod metuas labem meruisse tyranni
Cunctos si perimit sontes nunc poena repertos,
Crudelis, si mitis, eris; par opprimat aestus
Vltio pestiferos, tua quos prudentia mire
Auertit, superaque sinus cor luce refertum.
190   His grauiter dictis, sic regius incipit ardor;
Soli nostra salus summo aeternoque parenti
Debita sit, tantis eius clementia nullum
Laudibus admittit socium, atque immensa potestas
Effugisse sat est hostilia fulmina nobis,
Istos ingrati nequid meditemur honores.
Exorsus tali pius est sermone monarcha.
Verborum sed enim cur haud superabile flumen
Ingredior? cymbaque leui feror altus in aequor
Immensum, celsis mox exorbendus ab vndis?
200   Sic Phoebi puer egit equos, ita parua cicada
Exili tonitru Iouis assimulabit hiatu.
Pascua nam veluti cum ver infantibus ornat
Floribus, egelidae soluuntur in aethere nubes,
Et placide dulces succedunt imbribus imbres,
Nil saeui si non cogente Aquilone minantes:
Vocibus haud aliter iucundis ora liquescunt
Sceptriferi dicentis, et aurea flumina fundunt,
Quae modo si feruent facere hoc inuita videntur,
Flatibus et tanquam aduersis animata feruntur.
210   Ingratos prout et facili castigat abusos

And in what darkness would wretched Britain have mourned, bereft
of her sun, her moon and her lesser stars, with the removal of
the prince and the starlike girls? Who would have provided light
for the church, who would have artfully set in order the intrac-
table countryside, and imposed peace where there were arms? Who
would have settled suits in the lawcourts with a father's jus-
tice? Finally, what foresight would have guarded against foreign
attacks? If the plot prevailed what power was there to curb the
madness raging internally, or what comfort could then allay the
griefs of wives or mothers, if in a moment so great and so unex-
pected a disaster had fallen upon the Britons in the midst of
peace, all their ordinances put asunder as if by one lightning
stroke? Thus rages your fury O Rome, and the dread progeny of
Ignatius, of diabolic and ambiguous birth. O mildest of kings,
how far will you tolerate such ills? What bound will your ill
starred patience set? Now mildness is harmful, and unpunished
the evil will increase, until, too late to remedy, it has finally
turned into a disaster. It is not what you fear - that you have
merited the taint of tyrant if punishment destroys all those
found guilty. You will be cruel if you are kind. Let a punish-
ment fit for the crime overtake the rebellious uprising which
your wisdom miraculously averted, your heart illumined with light
from above."
     After these grave words, the king ardently speaks:
     "May the debt of our safety be owed solely to the eternal
father in the highest. His mercy does not admit of any companion
in these praiseworthy acts, and his immense power is sufficient
for us to have escaped the thunderbolts of the enemy. Let us not
reflect on those noble offices without gratitude".
     The pious monarch arose with this speech. But why do I
embark upon the innavigable stream of speech? Am I borne into
the immensity of the high seas on a light craft, soon to be
sucked under by the mighty waves? Thus did the boy drive the
horses of Phoebus, so did the little cicada in its tiny throat
try to emulate the thunder of Jove. Now just as when the spring
decorates the fields with infant flowers, the chilly snow clouds
dissolve in the heavens, and sweet showers gently follow on,
showers threatening nothing severe if not driven by the south
wind, just so did the lips of the king melt in sweet tones as he
spoke, and pour forth golden streams which if they ever rage do
so unwillingly, and are borne away as if driven by contrary
gales. Just so the king, provoked by the thunderous uprising,
chastises the Papist ingrates who have abused his easy goodness,

Papicolas bonitate sua rex concitus aestu
Fulmineo, nolensque ardet, dum saeua recenset
Prodigia, et tribus intentata pericula regnis
Per scelus, atque dolum, et quo nil violentius, ignem.
Irae non igitur reprimendae laxat habenas,
Sopitumque diu vagina diripit ensem,
Elata magnum dimittens voce senatum.
Tempus, ait, veteres nunc est defendere leges
Non reperire nouas; vindictam sumite, nostra
220   Iam nihil impediet clementia, victa recessit.
Quilibet ergo suas sedes petat, vndique sparsos
Supplicijs multate hostes, dignoque cruore
Eluite hance labem, ac terram purgate Britannam;
Dixit; prosequiturque abeuntem murmure laeto
Tota cohors, lenemque vocat iustumque Iacobum.
        Sed conspirati scelerum discussa suorum
Nubila cernentes, et nuda fronte patere
Coepta horrenda tremunt, turpes ceu Gorgones vnda
Cum se tranquilla aspiciunt, pudor et metus vrgent.
230   Ac veluti tragico cum turget scena cothurno,
Alcidesque furens agitur, fataleque Nessi
Induitur donum; fumat vel coena Thyestei;
Spectante Althea vel stipes luridus ardet:
Instruitur tristi crudelis fabula pompa,
Emergunt Cocyto vmbrae miseranda malorum
Omnia ructantes, proceditque vnus et alter
Belle actus; lachrimis turgessere lumina tandem
Spectantum incipiunt extremus vt aduenit horror,
Dum latera actores rumpunt, tanguntque coronam,
240   Sed mox deficiunt scena siue voce silenti,
Explosique moram metuunt, latebrasque petiscunt:
Sic vbi summa operis, messisque, et palma vocaret
Ad praedam coniuratos, et saeua trophaea,
Fornice detecto mutescunt; obuia passim
Sanguineae Nemesis disclusos terret imago,
Credunt iam tenebris potius quam viribus vllis
Vitas incertas, et spes; mediaeque sub vmbra
Noctis Lambethi coeunt, euentaque voluunt.
Conqueritur primo Vritus; quid doemonis atri
250   Protulit occultum facinus? namque haud deus, inquit,
Sanctorumue aliquis tam pulchros proderet ausus:
Occidimus; spes, o socij, jam corruit ingens,
Et meriti decus in lachrimas vanescit, et vmbras.
Quem portum petimus? votis contrarius Auster

and unwillingly grows heated as he reviews   the cruel monstrosi-
ties and perils directed at the triple kingdom through wickedness
of treachery and fire,   than which nothing could be more violent.
He therefore does not check the reins of his anger,   and snatches
the sword that has long slept in its scabbard,   dismissing the
mighty council with his raised voice:

"It is   now time to defend our old laws, not to find new
ones; take vengeance;   our mercy will not hinder at all - van-
quished it gives ground. Whoever makes for home, visit them with
the vengeance due to an enemy who has scattered far and wide, and
with righteous blood wash clean this stain, and purge the land of
Britain."

He spoke. As he left the whole troop followed him with joy-
ous murmur, and called James mild and just.

But the conspirators,   seeing the cover of their wicked
actions gone tò the winds and that their abominable attempt is
laid naked to view, shudder like foul Gorgons when they see them-
selves reflected in the smooth water;   shame and fear press in
upon them.   And just as when the stage swells to tragic strains,
and Hercules is driven mad and wears the fatal gift of Nessus, or
when the banquet of Thyestes reeks,   or when, as Althea watches,
the brand burns with ghastly glow; a cruel plot is constructed
with solemn ceremony,   shades from Cocytus emerge belching forth
all the pitiable sufferings of evildoers, one act proceeds to the
next beautifully, at the end the eyes of the spectators begin to
swell with tears as the final horror approaches, while the actors
break their sides and touch the crowd, but soon they leave the
stage with silent voice, or hissed off the stage,   they fear a
halt to the proceedings, and try to seek cover:- so when the com-
pletion of their task, its harvest and the palm,   should have
called the conspirators to their spoil and their cruel trophies,
when the vault is discovered, they become silent, and on all
sides the image of an appalling Nemesis confronts them in terror.
They entrust their uncertain lives and hopes now to concealment
rather than to any effort. Under the cover of midnight, they
come together at Lambeth and turn over the outcome. First Wright
complains:

"What dark action of the devil brought the hidden deed to
light, for not God or any one of the saints would have discovered
so fair an enterprise?   We are lost. Our great hope is now in
ruins, and the splendour of our meritorious act vanishes into
tears and shadows. What haven do we seek? A south wind, con-
trary to our prayers, has thrown our intended journey into confu-

Propositum turbauit iter, coelumque procellis
Vndique crudescit, Syrtes, atque aspera saxa
Obiectans oculis, Scillasque et mille Charibdes.
Armis nulla salus, nec si fuga forte deceret
Tam sublime ausos quicquam prodesset, vbique
260   Ignotus speculator adest, quotque ora tot hostes
Aspicimus; certam promittunt omnia cladem.
Tardius aut citius genitum quodcunque peribit
Percius exclamat, liceat mortalibus esse,
Nec coepti nos poeniteat, nec sortis iniquae:
Quod nequeas mutare feras; non omnibus vnum
Impendet fatum, impendet tamen omnibus vnum.
Sic iter ingressus coelo fortasse sereno
Perpetuam per planitiem sterilemque viator,
Non illic hominum apparent, non tecta ferarum,
270   Non virgultum humilem nec dumus proijcit vmbram;
Terra Ioui patet omnis, et irascentibus Euris;
Ille via laetatur adhuc, radijsque benignis,
Aetheris at si sit facies mutata repente,
Si fulmen tonitruque fremant, premat imbribus Auster
Quid faciat miser? incoeptum num deserat ergo
Exanimatus iter? reliquum imperterritus omni
Conatu an peraget, feret et quae ferre necesse est?
Deficiente dolo, quid in considimus armis?
Virtutem exacuant nunc ipsa pericula nostram
280   Bellum finis erat, quo nondum vtamur adempto.
Percius arma, fugam laudat Vinterus et aptam
Pollicitus nauem dubio praeponit honesto
Vtile, quod certam possit spondere salutem.
Quo tandem, aut ad quos fugientia tendimus, inquit,
Vela Catisbaeus? quos imploremus amicos?
Anne illos quorum vano molimine causam
Perdidimus? temere quorum violauimus aras?
Coepta peracta licet grata et speciosa fuissent
Nostra, infecta odium parient, spretisque pudorem:
290   Quin aliquod demum factum edimus, imus ad arma,
Sic non indecores, sic non moriemur inulti.
Haec fato furiali omnes arma, arma tumultu
Ingeminant, tollunt animos virtute coacta.
Ceu cum nulla fugae reliqua est via, nulla saluti,
Obuertunt cerui canibus se, in cornua surgunt,
Et sine spe tremulo contra luctamine tendunt.
Maxima consilij vis ad noua bella cienda
Est data Iesuitis, eadem quos culpa prophanis
Miscet, et eiusdem stimulat mens conscia causae.
300   Nocte igitur praemissus eques luctum explicat omnem

sion, and heaven grows violent on every side with storms, pre-
senting before our eyes Syrtes, rugged rocks, and a thousand
Scyllas and Charybdes.   There is no salvation in arms, nor if
flight could perhaps become those who have attempted acts of such
sublime daring would it have been of any profit; everywhere is
some unknown spy.   All the faces we look upon are enemies; all
things hold promise of disaster."

"Sooner or later every mortal thing created will perish"
(interjects Percy) "make this allowance to mortality, nor let us
repent of our attempt, or our unjust lot.   What you cannot
change, you must bear.   Not over everybody does the one fate
hang, but one nevertheless hangs over all.   And so perhaps a
traveller starts his journey through a never ending desert plain
under a clear sky; no men are seen there, nor cover for wild
beast, no thicket or bramble throws out its shade on the ground;
the whole land lies open to the sky and the angry Easterlies; he
still rejoices in his journey and in sun's beneficent rays, but
if the face of heaven should suddenly be changed, if thunder and
lightning strike, and the south wind pursues him with rain, what
is the wretched man to do? Does he therefore abandon the journey
that he has begun, fainthearted?   Or will he carry on with the
remainder unperturbed at every trial, and bear what it is neces-
sary to bear?   Now that the plot fails, why do we rest upon our
arms? Let our peril itself whet our courage. The end was open
war, which has not been taken away from us and which we may yet
use."

Percy praises arms, Winter flight, and puts expediency which
could guarantee safety before an honourable course which is of
doubtful outcome.

"Whither or to whom in the end do we turn our fugitive
sails" (asks Catesby) "what friends are we to call upon for aid?
Those whose cause we lost in our vain manoevre?   Those whose
altars we rashly desecrated?   Though in success our endeavours
would have brought us gratitude and glory, in failure they will
breed hatred and shame for us who are spurned.   Why do we not
rather do some final deed, resort to arms, and so we will not die
dishonourably or unavenged."

After this passionate speech they all renew the call to arms
with a roar, and raise their spirits with forced courage, just as
when there is no way left for flight and none for safety, stags
turn themselves to face the dogs, they rear up to buck with their
antlers and contend without hope in fearful resistance.   The
greatest authority was given to the advice of the Jesuits in the
matter of raising any new combats (the Jesuits who bear equal
blame for these profanities and who are motivated by minds com-
mitted to the same cause).   At night therefore a rider is des-
patched to explain the sad state of affairs to Garnet, and the

Garneto, extremo in casu decretaque bella.
Ille metu trepidans socios arcessit, acerba
Praescripti degustata nouitate pericli
Exacuens prius, obtusis mora ne quid obesset.
 Conuenere patres, venerabile nomine solo
Concilium, nam voce metum vultuque fatentur
Pertimidi, primis nec adhaerent proxima verba.
Tandem Garneti effundit se viribus auctis
Copia solliciti sed et haec quoque plena timoris.
310 Heu quantis nos foeta malis sors obsidet, inquit,
O socij, ah metuo hinc noster iam funditus ordo
Ne cadat, abruptique gemat sub pondere coepti.
Vsque adeo indignam sapit, et quam quilibet horret
Barbariem, licet hoc aliam fortasse peractum
Indueret speciem, commutaretque colorem,
Quodque atrum nunc conspicitur remearet in album.
Quis fidei pactae oblitus nostrique suique,
Indicium dedit extrema emolitus in hora
Infoelix animaeque suae, nostraeque saluti?
320 Sed tam dira deo credo molimina nunquam
Sat placuisse, aliud prorsum clementia patris
Aetherei exposcit, miserorum animusque misertus.
Quid memorem extinctae plusquam miranda misellae
Reginae effugia? exemplo mihi sufficit vnus
Interpres verax nimium, nimiumque benigno
Afflatu adiutus, scriptum qui debile vertit
Nostram in pernitiem, frustra quam tendimus illi.
Insidias nondum natus contempsit, et ipsis
In cunis magno potuit plus Hercule, binos
330 Quem manibus colubros extinguere Graecia fingit.
Iupiter huic fertur pater et patronus, at illi est
Verus, et omnipotens, et ad omnia numine praesens.
Res magis euentis cur censes increpat Hallus
Quam recta ratione pater? diuina voluntas
Quas acies olim instruxit bis fuderat hostis,
Peiores igitur tibi, contemptaeque videntur?
Pulsus et a Turcis rex Gallicus, an minor ergo
Causa, vt sorte fuit? num classica digna triumpho
Quae capta cecinere Rhode, aut meliora putemus,
340 Obsessos quod iniqua pios victoria spreuit?
Nobis fas, nostrae non est diffidere causae.
Haec disceptari Gerrardus tempore tali,
Tesmundusque vetant, sibi nunc opus esse suisque,
Mox vt succurrant re, consilio, auxilioque,
Arma mouenda premunt, nec in his mora tuta mouendis.

decision to resort to arms in their calamity.   Trembling with
fear, he summons his comrades, first goading them into action by
touching lightly upon the bitter news of the peril that had been
communicated by letter, in case delay caused by their sluggish-
ness should further damage them.

The fathers convened a council reverend in name only, for
fear in voice and expression declares their alarm, and their
speech is disjointed. At length Garnet pours himself out in agi-
tation to their assembled numbers, but his oratory too is full of
fear.

"Alas, how does fate besiege us newly delivered of such
great ills, my comrades.   O I am afraid that our order, groaning
under the weight of this unsuccessful enterprise may collapse
completely, so greatly does it ever savour of that wild severity,
from which everyone recoils, though it is possible that this out-
come might take on a different complexion and change its colour,
and what now appears black might change back to white.   Who was
it who, forgetful of the pact of our and his faith, unhappily
exercised in the final hour of trial for his soul and for our
salvation, gave information? But such endeavours I believe never
sufficiently pleased God;   and indeed the mercy of our heavenly
Father and a soul that has compassion for those who suffer demand
some other remedy.   Why should I recall more than the wondrous
escapes of the poor wretched queen now dead?   as exemplary proof
sufficient for me is that fact of that single interpreter too
revealing of the truth, and helped by too benificent an inspira-
tion, who turned the feeble writing and the destruction we are
vainly aiming at him into our own ruin.   He spurned our plotting
even before he was born and in the cradle itself could accomplish
more than Hercules who in Greek legend strangled two snakes with
his bare hands.   Jupiter is said to be his father and protector,
but with James it is He who is true, all powerful, and present at
everything with his power."

"Why do you judge of things more in results than in the
rightness of their cause, father?" exclaims Hall in rebuke.
"Those forces which the will of God had drawn up together in the
past the enemy had twice routed - do they seem inferior to you
and contemptible for that?   The French king was driven back by
the Turks - was he therefore worsted in his cause as he was in
his fate?   Surely we do not think those trumpets which were
sounded at the capture of Rhodes worthy of triumph and more sim-
ply because a victory destroyed the besieged, a triumph of evil
over good?   It is not right for us not to have confidence in our
own cause."

Gerard and Tesimond do not allow the dispute to continue at
such a time.   Their direct need now was to help themselves and
their fortune, to rescue the situation with a plan and practical
help. They press for the move to arms to be made. Delay in mak-

Garnetus nondum quassato robore regni,
Rege vigente, in vindictam populoque furente,
Difficile esse armis contra contendere suadet.
Hallus huic haeret parti, nec conuenit illis
350 Inter se, variat dubias sententia mentes.
Ex improuiso attonitis sese obijcit vmbra
Ignati, tristi aspectu, saeuumque minanti;
Olim qualis erat, cum publica castra sequendo
Fessus militiae valedixit, et ordinis author
Esse noui voluit, metuit nec nomen abuti
Audito quo terra tremit, quo sternitur Orcus:
Hisque ferus pauidos incessit vocibus vltro.
Vnde animis tantus labor? eccum Ignatius adsum
Loyola, patronumque ducemque agnoscite vestrum.
360 Ah pudet o socij vel vos Phlegetonte vomenti
Terrores flecti, nostrum pallere nefas sit.
Vos pedibus regum par est capita aurea vestris
Calcare, atque omnes rerum contemnere casus,
Aduersis etiam pandentes vela procellis.
Magno equidem incaepto laudem meruisse fatebor
Ingentem vtcumque est voto fraudata voluntas:
Quod lepide modo cessisset, fataleque puluis
Fecerat officium, sparsusque senatus in auras
Fulmine Romano totus cum rege perisset,
370 O quantum decus hinc? qualis mihi fama, meisque
Iure affulsisset? magnum vt terroribus orbem
Noster adimplesset cunctis mirabilis ordo?
Gloria sed nobis se inuidit tanta, suosque
Nectare quos aluit spes felle fefellit alumnos.
Vtraque nunc igitur valeat dea, spes noua vestris
Mentibus accedat, noua gloria laeta sequetur.
Arma animis versate, nec his dolus exulet armis:
Principio passim rumores spargite vanos,
Papicolasque metu caedis terrete futurae:
380 Impendere illis communem fingite cladem,
Occulte peragi rem, maturamque minari
Vim subitam, nisi vi contra maturius itur.
Vocibus interea vosmet spaciosius ipsis
Currite circumquaque, recurrite, et vndique notos
Sollicitate viros, miserisque implete querelis
Foemineum genus, immensi loca cuncta onerate
Suspicione mali, nihil vt sit tutius armis.
Ipse ego Tartareosque Metus Furiasque ciebo,
Diras, atque imis quicquid saeui abditur vmbris.
390 Vix ea fatus erat, subtus cum terra dehiscens

ing this move is dangerous.   Garnet,   since the strength of the
realm was as yet unshaken, with the king in health and the people
raging for vengeance,   urges that it is difficult to fight back
with arms. Hall clings to his side, nor is there agreement among
them; opinion divides their doubtful minds.   Suddenly to their
astonished eyes, the ghost of Ignatius appears, of gloomy aspect
and severely threatening, such as once he was when, weary of fol-
lowing a soldier's life, he bid farewell to the military and made
a vow to be the founder of a new order, nor does he fear to take
advantage of the name at the mention of which the earth trembles,
and Hell is prostrate.   Unbidden he fiecely assails them as they
quail with these words:
     "Whence all this labour of soul?   Behold Ignatius Loyola; I
am come. Recognise your patron and general.   It is shameful, O
comrades,   that you be moved when Phlegethon vomits up its ter-
rors.   For our sort to grow pale may it ever be a crime.   It is
one and the same to you to trample the golden heads of kings
under your feet, and to have scorn for all eventualities, unfur-
ling your sails even in the teeth of gales. I shall acknowledge
that great praise has been earned by that mighty undertaking,
howsoever the wish of our prayers was cheated. Would that it had
only gone smoothly and the powder had done its fatal task, and
the whole council together with the king had been scattered
through the air by a Roman thunderbolt and perished.   O what
glory from this?   What fame would rightly have flowed to me and
mine, so that our wondrous order might fill the world with every
terror?   But such great glory begrudged itself to us and cheated
its devotees with poison whom hope had nourished with nectar.
Now therefore may both goddesses be strong, may fresh hope enter
your hearts, fresh glory will joyfully follow. Turn your minds
to arms, and let not these arms be without treachery.   In the
first place spread vain rumours everywhere.   Terrify the catho-
lics with fear of slaughter to come. Invent a disaster common to
all of them: say the thing is being planned secretly, sudden and
early violence threatens unless forestalled by earlier force. In
the meantime yourselves hasten round even more widely than the
rumours you spread, here there and every where, retrace your
steps again, and make overtures to all men known to you every-
where, and fill the female sex with complaints, burden all places
with the suspicion of a great enormity, so that nothing seems
safer than arms.   I myself will raise hellish fears and dreadful
furies, and whatever savage thing is hidden in deepest darkness."
     Scarcely had he spoken when the earth opening up from under-

Pandit Auernales flammis crepitantibus vndas;
Misceturque suis Ignatius; omnia turbans
Aduentu primo; Dirarum nomina rauca
Voce tonat, trepidosque Metus vocat, excitat omnes
Impiger e cauejs Furias, ignobilis addens
Horribilem vulgi numero sine, et ordine turbam.
Sic aciem instructam superas agit acer in auras,
Ignitum quatiens dextra, intentansque flagellum,
Tartareo spectante, suo nec poenitet ipsum
400   Cedere jam de iure pari, vnum pectus vtrisque est.
Visa sed haec oculis spectantum excussa repente
Restituere solum, diuulsaque Tartara claudunt.
Terruit, ac merito, patres mirabile spectrum,
Et consternatis si non Ignatius illas
Firmasset, rigido mentes horrore fugasset.
Omnia sed [tumidis animis] despecta minori
[Iam facie] apparent; Alcides maximus illis
Antaeum attollens Pigmaeus cum grue certans
Vix foret, aut gestans lactentem simia pupum;
410   Flumine sic atro turgent, ita sceptra sacrata
Et regum elati prae se diademata temnunt,
Heroes nunc orbe noui, ac domini dominantum.
Iamque exclusa Erebo furiarum maxima bellum
Quae serit, et cui regnorum discordia cordi est,
Flammam Iesuitis Stygiam ceu fulmen in ora
Conijcit, ima petit vesanus viscera feruor.
Praecipitesque agitat diuersos, arma frementes,
Implentesque sacris sua classica dira susurris.
Verum accendenti maiori lampade martem
420   Garneto, occurrit peracuta armata securi
Immensaque ferox Nemesis, taboque madenti,
Intentamque aciem vibrans haec intonat ore:
Cur bellum concire opera contendis inani
Vecors, aut fatis vltra te opponere tentas?
Plus satis admisti sceleris, tua perdita facta
Prodita iam poenam exposcunt quam sanguine solues,
Nec tua multorum marcescens vita dierum est.
Externam malefidus opem, ne credulus erres,
[Distrahit] Oceanus, procul hinc tibi Roma vocanti,
430   Quid coelum? magnis coelum si sontibus vllum est.
Talia vaticinata fugit velut vmbra, relinquens
Exanimem, mortisque metu prope jam morientem.
    At scelera his tandem lucem didicere magistris
Ferre, palam coeunt turbae, atque hostilia tentant.
Aedes inuadunt alienas, limina clausa

neath reveals the waters of Avernus with their crackling flames, and Ignatius mixes amongst them, disturbing them all in his first plunge. He thunders out the names of the Dire Ones in a raucous voice, calls up trembling Fears, and quickly rouses all the Furies from their caves, ignobly adding a horrid crew, undistinguished in number or kind. He assembles and keenly drives this troop into the upper air, brandishing a fiery weapon in his right arm, and threatening with his whip, as the Infernal One watches; nor is he sorry to yield from equal command, for they both have one heart. But Ignatius gazes on all these sights which are suddenly snatched from the vision of the spectators. His ministers have restored the earth and are closing up Hell. This stupendous spectacle terrifies the fathers, and rightly, and if Ignatius had not given them strength in their consternation, it would have driven them out of their minds in its stark horror. But everything to their overweening spirits now appeared contemptible and on a reduced scale; to their eyes the most mighty Hercules lifting Antaeus would scarcely be a pigmy fighting with a crane, or a monkey carrying a suckling child. Thus they swell with the dark tide, and in comparison with themselves, now the new heroes of the earth, they loftily disdain the sacred sceptres and crowns of kings and exercise dominion as lords. And now let out from Hell the greatest of the Furies who raises wars and whose heart is warmed by the clashing of kingdoms, hurls upon the Jesuits Stygian fire like a thunderbolt into their faces. The maddening heat seeks their innermost vital parts, and drives them headlong in all directions, raging after arms, giving with holy whisperings substance to their dread alarums. To Garnet, truly kindling war now with a keener torch, there appeared armed with a razor-sharp axe a huge and frightening Nemesis with an oozing infection, and darting her piercing gaze, she thunders thus in speech:
   "Why do you strive to raise war with this vain labour, foolish man? Or are you trying to oppose the fates beyond your power? You have mixed in transgression more than enough. Your baleful doings now brought to light demand punishment which you will pay with your blood, nor has your life many days left as it withers away. The untrustworthy ocean cuts off aid from abroad, in case you trustingly should be in any doubt about it, as you call upon Rome far from here. What of heaven? If there is any heaven for great sinners."
   Uttering such in prophetic tones, she fled like a shadow, leaving him faint, and now nearly dying of the fear of death. But under such masters crimes learn to bear the light. Openly they band together, and begin hostilities. They invade the

Vi penetrant, rapiunt in fortia praelia doctos
Sicubi equos, vetitisque trahunt de postibus arma.
Illis vrbani, maior quos concitat ardor,
Assiduo socij miscentur, et vndique crescunt.
440 Aequore tranquillo ceu quando inopina virescit
Tempestas, ruit hinc Notus, hinc ferus inuolat Eurus,
Tolluntur fluctus paulatim, nubila coelo
Se produnt magis atque magis iam iamque timere
Incipiunt nautae sibi, diuitbusque carinis.
Sic etiam subitis cum rura tumultibus ardent
(Alta quibus facilisque quies assueuerat olim)
Quasque magis metuit plebs quam sua numina leges
Contemni, nihilique videt nunc esse, furori
Cedere ius, ferroque geri rem; quisque minatur
450 Naufragium sibi, se vix tectis aut sua credit.
Gens ita nunc natis horret Cornauia turbis
Perpetuos quorum placide praeterfluit agros
Dulcis Auona, ortu, decursuque aemula solis.
Ante alios annis grauis, ingenioque Greuillus
[Turbida cui ceu custodi] prouincia cessit,
Rumores varios spargi, admittique rapinas
Audit, nil magni, nil tanto at nomine dignum.
Vultu sed Stygiam dum vim fugat aethere ab alto
Sidereus iuuenis, subtus tremit imaque turma,
460 Ceu sternuntur aues aquila volitante minores,
Aspicit ecce senem cunctantem, animoque futura
Delibantem, igitur densa nube vndique tectus
Aduolat, et roseis digitis simul eximit vnum
Ex illis radijs circum aurea tempora qui stant
Perpetuum in sertum glomerantes, sideris instar:
Ille, viri dextrum, jubar hoc jaculatus, ocellum
Percutit, auratisque petit summa aethera pennis.
Protinus horrescit coelesti percitus ictu
Mortalis, sentit maiori lumine totum
470 Perfundi caput, et pectus; videt omnia multo
Acrius, atque sapit, praesentia, siue futura.
Quos modo contempsit rumores, nunc timet; ante
Dicta audita simul trutinata lance coercens.
Principia haud ita magna graues portendere motus
Aestimat interea, quos vel componere miti
Arte parat, vel vi stimulata extinguere saltem.
Cogitat ingentes quandoque existere flammas
Parua ex scintilla quia sit neglecta furenti,
Cauta vel in minimis prodest vigilantia rebus.
480 Non bene custodita suae primum ergo redegit

houses of strangers, break through closed doors, seize from any-
where horses trained for battle, and from forbidden door-posts
drag down arms.   City dwellers whom greater passions rouse con-
tinually join with them as comrades, and from all quarters num-
bers increase.   Just as when on a calm sea a sudden storm begins
to grow, hither rushes the south wind, hither flies the fierce
easterly, little by little the waves are whipped up, clouds show
themselves more and more in the sky, and now ever increasingly
the sailors begin to fear for themselves and their rich holds;
even so the country areas, where formerly had reigned a wide-
spread and easy calm are inflamed with sudden uproars, and the
common people see the laws, which they fear more than their own
deities, slighted and counting for nought. Justice yields before
madness.   Matters are decided by the sword.   Every man fears
shipwreck for himself and scarcely trusts himself and his belong-
ings to his house.   So now the people of the midlands shrink from
the disturbances now rising, whose age-old fields the sweet Avon
gently flows by like the rising or the setting of the sun.
Reverend before others in age and wisdom, Greville, to whose pro-
tection the disturbed province was committed, hears that various
rumours are spreading and robberies taking place, but nothing of
great moment or worth any great name.   But while, starlike in
countenance, the youth from heaven above puts the hellish power
to flight, and the lowest crowd below are cowering in fear, just
as when the eagle flies lesser birds quail, lo and behold he sees
the old man hesitating and only perceiving in his mind a little
of what is to come, and therefore in a thick cloud, covered on
all sides, he flies down, and with his rosy fingers straightway
plucks one of those rays which always encircle his golden temples
in an everlasting garland, like a star.   Casting this beam, he
pierces the right eye of the old man, and makes for the highest
heavens on golden wings.   Directly the mortal man shudders,
pierced by this shot from heaven; he feels his whole head and
heart being bathed in greater light, he sees all things present
or things to come.   The rumours that he had thought little of he
now fears, duly weighing words heard before in balanced scale.
In the meantime he judges that beginnings not in themselves so
important portend serious upheavals which he prepares either to
settle with gentle persuasion, or to put an end to with force
raised for the occasion.   He reflects that at some time or other
great fires spring from the raging of a tiny spark because it has
been neglected, and even in the smallest matters a careful vigi-
lance is profitable.   Therefore he reclaims those arms which had

G

Arma potestati, fortes sermone bonosque
Prudenti exacuens, quosque aut fortuna genusue
Extulit hortatur memorans sortemque genusque.
At patriae cunctos communi incendit amore,
Aspergens odio turbas probrisque rebelles:
Excultaeque adeo valuit facundia linguae
Vt contempti hostes, desertique ocius vltro
Diffugiant, quam vis neque deses cogere posset.
Praetereunt celeres faecundae pascua Auonae,
490   Aduersisque alte nemora assurgentia ripis,
Inque tuis fessi tandem Sabrina residunt
Vicinis campis; ast omnem hance excipit vna
Colluuiem priuata domus quam debilis ardor
Nequicquam munire parat pugnaque tueri.
Holbechi retinet nomen locus, haud malus, huius
Conscius hospitij quod erat, si fama taceret.
      Ecce autem nunquam fidus, nulloque ligandus
Pacto Tartareus, quos sustulit ante beatos,
Nunc odio miseros necat, atque vt inutile pondus
500   Abijcit, impendentem amat accelerare ruinam.
Funereas igitur Dirarum immittit in aedes
Vnam, sed maestis aptam, summeque nocinam.
Deiectis datur illa comes, noctesque diesque
Assidet horrorem incutiens, et tristia visa
Praetendens, animisque aegris fastidia vitae
Suadet, et immaturo obiectat corpora Letho.
Occultae rerum naturae gnara, trementes
(O sacrum artificem) venas succo imbuit atro
Inuoluens tenebris mentem, peioraque spectris
510   Somnia sopitis, noctem vigilantibus infert.
Huic pesti infoelix est desperatio nomen,
Illa remollitos curis quae perdit amantes,
Dedecore afflictos, vel paupertate grauatos,
Siue fruendarum quos cepit nausea rerum;
Lubrica pernicies, tabe exitiosior omni,
Non aliena tamen nunc, aptaque talibus hospes.
Vinterum fratri quem sors mutata minori
Exequat, cultu spoliatum, reque paterna
In somnis dira aggreditur praesagaque veris
520   Territat ominibus jucundae inimica quieti.
Templorum erectos obeliscos aere tonantes
Interualla cauo obliquos, velutique ruentes
Ostendit; sacrisque aditis (quae visus adire est)
Horribiles vultus praefert, quos nec bene nouit
Nec prorsum ignorat dubie miser omnia cernens

not been well protected for his own power, encouraging the brave
and the good by wise speech, and heartening those whom fortune or
their lineage had singled out, reminding them of their lineage
and lot.   But he inflamed all with a common love of their coun-
try, showering the rebels with reproaches and the troublesome
mobs with ill will.   The eloquence of his polished tongue was so
powerful that the enemy, disdained and deserted, fled of their
own accord faster than the swiftest force could have compelled
them.   They quickly pass by the pastures of the fruitful Avon and
the woods that rise on its banks on either side, and at length
wearily settle in your neighbouring fields, Sabrina.   But a sin-
gle private house takes in all this draff, which a failing pas-
sion in vain prepares to fortify and protect from the fray.   The
place keeps the name of Holbeche, scarcely evil because it was
guilty of this hospitality, if fame were to keep it silent.

But behold Satan, never to be trusted and never to be bound
to any pact, now kills those whom he had previously sustained in
success now that they are abject and hated, and casts them off
like a useless burden.   He loves to hasten an impending disaster.
He therefore sends into the house of death a single Fury, but one
most fit for the sorrowful, and hurtful in the extreme.   She is
sent as a companion to the dejected, and night and day she sits
by their side inflicting her terror, and feigning gloomy
visions, and she urges a loathing for life upon sickened souls
and throws bodies to death before their time.   Knowing hidden
secrets of nature, she can fill trembling veins with a dark
potion (a sacred art) perplexing the mind with obscurity, and she
brings dreams worse than spectres to those asleep, and the dark-
ness of night to those awake.   Despair is the unhappy name of
this fiend; she who destroys lovers made tender by cares, or
those afflicted with disgrace, or burdened with poverty, or sick-
ened by a surfeit of pleasure; a slimy pest, more deadly than any
wasting disease, but to such men no foreign visitor, and now most
fit.   Winter, now spoiled of his honour and his inherited wealth,
whom fortune had made equal to his younger brother, the dread
Fury now assails and terrifies in sleep, presaging with true
omens, the enemy of sweet rest.   She shows steeples raised in
churches thundering tones from their echoing bronze, bending and
in the act of falling.   On the sacred entrance (which he seems to
approach) she fixes terrible faces which he neither knew well,
nor was wholly ignorant of.   As he surveyed all in doubt and mis-

Conceptoque metu perfundit tempora sudor.
Sed noua sollicitos Lux, et cita tympana somnos
Excutiunt, subito tenues nam milite muros
Valseus obsedit, pulsa qui pelle sonora
530   Verba interclusos ad mutua prouocat hostes
Tum pacem, ac veniae spem desertoribus offert
Ignarus scelerum tantorum; at conscia turba
Oblata irridens vim contra se ocius armat.
Aptant horrisona in pugnam tormenta, propinquum
Puluis et humescens nimium nitrosus ad ignem
Siccatur, sed lenta foco dum ligna minister
Suscitat, ecce manum (nulli conspecta) trementis
Dira rapit, prunasque nigra commiscet arena.
Concipit haec cito flammam, et tecti (fulminis instar)
540   Culmine pertuso erumpit, semustaque turpat
Ora virum, tetra confundens omnia nocte.
Sed simul exclusis nidoribus alma diei
Lux redit, horrificosque datur distinguere vultus;
En hos Vinterus clamat, nempe hos ego vidi
In somnis vultus, irae heu nimis omnia vera
Diuinae? heu nostris quam digna incendia coeptis?
Flexis jamque omnes genibus per vulnera tecti
Ad coelum palmas, atque ora immania tendunt,
Horrendo veniam incoepto, pacemque precantes.
Dira sed hanc propere pietatem auertit, ad aures
550   Tympana mille sonans placidas simulata per auras.
Surgit ad arma cohors, portisque patentibus exit,
Haud vincendi spe, studio sed mortis honestae.
Contra contendit crudo cum milite Valseus.
Percius occursu primo, et cadit ictus eadem
Glande Catisbaeus, iuxtaque Vritus vterque
Purpureas fundunt animas; sed Granta, Rucodes,
Vinterique ambo capti ducuntur ab hoste;
Et Batus et Caius; multum nec dispare fato
Poenas mox omnes merito cum sanguine soluunt.

ery, and as he felt fear, sweat poured round his temples.   But a
fresh dawn and sudden drumbeats dispelled their troubled sleep,
for with a sudden force Walsh was laying seige to their weak
walls, who, after striking the sounding skin, called the enemy
enclosed within to an exchange of words.   Then unaware of the
greatness of their crimes, he offers peace and hope of pardon to
the renegades.   But the guilty mob, mocking the offerings of the
man, armed themselves against him with speed.   They set up their
terrible sounding engines for battle.   Nitric powder, too damp,
is dried by the fire nearby, but while a servant rouses the slow
wood in the hearth, lo and behold an invisible Fury seizes the
hand of the trembling man, and intermingles burning coals with
the black sand.   This quickly seizes the flame, and like a thun-
derbolt explodes, making a hole in the top of the roof, and it
besmirches the halfscorched faces of the men, plunging everybody
into a foul darkness.   But as soon as the bountiful light of day
returns, the noxious fumes dispelled, and it is possible to make
out their dreadful faces.

      "Behold, these are the faces" exclaims Winter, "these are
indeed the faces I have seen in my dreams.   Alas are all these
manifestations of God's anger too true? Alas, how worthy is this
conflagration of our enterprise."

      And now all on their knees protected by their wounds, they
direct their hands and their monstrous faces to heaven, asking
for pardon for their abominable enterprise, and praying for
peace. But the Fury hastily turns their piety aside, sounding in
their ears a thousand imaginary drumbeats through the peaceful
air.   The troop rises to arms and goes out of the opening gates,
hardly in hope of victory, but in eagerness for an honourable
death.   Against them fights Walsh with his untrained force.
Percy falls in the first onslaught, and, struck by the same lead
ball Catesby falls, and side by side the two Wrights pour out
their bloodstained souls.   But Grant, Rookwood and both Winters
are led away captive by their enemy, as are Bates and Keyes.
There is not much difference in their fate.   Soon they all
rightly pay the penalty with death.

NOTES

Dedication

Throughout the transcription [ ] indicates a correction slip.
The pasted-over dedication to James reads as follows: ([ ] here
indicates uncertain readings; . . . indicates illegible letters)

> Potentissimo serenissimoque Jacobo
> Magnae Britanniae Franciae &c
> Hiberniae regi &c

Triumphanti hodie tibi (inuictissime Monarcha) serena
affulgeat quinta Novembris lux redeat vero quot=
annis ad laetitiam ad salutem ad gloriam. Opusculum
hoc quo dei opt: max: infinita bonitas vestrae autem diuinae
Prudentiae in puluerea coniuratione relegenda foelicitas cele=
brata est absolutum iam sub hac faustissima luce sacris tuis
manibus offerre haud ineptum fore judicem. Accipe igitur
clementissime potentissimeque patrone plusquam ..quis forsan aeui
munusculum, viuatius futurum si in [1..s..] exeunti vestra
benignitas inspirauerit[.] Viue quam diutissime[;] perpetuo vale,
foeliciter impera, sic nunc vt semper precatur.

> Vestrae maiestati
> humillime addictus

> Tho: Campianus

> (To the most powerful and serene James
> King of Great Britain, France, etc.,
> Scotland, etc.,

For you in triumph today (O most invincible King) may the light
of November the fifth shine serenely. Indeed may it return every
year to your joy, to your safety and to your glory. Allow me to
judge that it will not be inept to put into your sacred hands
this little work released now on this most auspicious day, this
little work in which is celebrated the infinite goodness of the
most excellent almighty God and on the other hand the felicity of

your divine wisdom in removing the gunpowder plot. Accept there-
fore, most merciful and most powerful protector, this little gift
that will perhaps have a longer life and more vitality if your
kindness has breathed favour upon it as it goes forth. Live for
as long as possible; perpetually farewell. Rule with good for-
tune; this now and ever be our prayer.

Most humbly dedicated to your majesty

Tho. Campion.)

Epigram 1

1.   'Roman wolves'. The depiction of Catholic priests and Jesuits
     as wolves, derived from Matthew, vii. 15, was one of the
     commonest epithets of abuse.

6.   'German shepherd'. Luther.

8.   To depict Jesuits as foxes was conventional. (Garnet is so
     called later in the text, at I. 354.) For 'vain tails' cf.
     Coke in Relation: "they are all ioyned in the tailes like
     Sampsons Foxes" (Sig. I3 r-v).

14-15.'The third time'. This is unclear; it may refer to the Hen-
     rician Reformation, the Elizabethan restoration and the Gun-
     powder Plot, or to the three plots against James, the 'By',
     'Main' and 'Gunpowder' Plots, or to three celebrated victo-
     ries - the Armada, the Gowrie Plot and the Gunpowder Plot.

Epigram 2

This and the next epigram play with the fact that the Jesu-
its adopted aliases to avoid detection. Garnet, the Jesuit
Superior, is the subject of Epigram 3, and at his trial it
was said "hee was a man Multorum Nominum but not boni Nomi-
num, of many names, as appeared by the Indictment, but of no
good Name" (Relation, Sig. O1r); cf. Robert Tynely, Two
Learned Sermons (1609): "For whereunto tendeth it, that one

Iesuite must bee called by so many names? . . . Is it not,
that going masked vnder so many names, as vnder so many
visards hee may the more securely lay his snares to entrap
vs?" (p. 6). The names which Campion coins are, again,
entirely typical of the standard abuse of the Jesuits.

Epigram 4

For a parallel sentiment, see the typical expression by W.
Leigh: "In stead of blowing vs up, they haue blowne vp
themselues, & their Religion, with such a wound to their
Cause, as will neuer be cured by any craft" (Great Britaines
Great Deliverance, 1606), Sig. C2r.

Epigram 5

This is a teasing epigram. The wit of it depends upon the
similarity of sounds in different syntactical elements in
Latin and English and is therefore wholly lost in transla-
tion.   The key seems to be a play upon the adverb duntaxat
(often dumtaxat in classical Latin, but here in its alterna-
tive form to harmonise with the spelling of John Donne's
name, "Dun") and upon the construction dun (an alternative
spelling of dum meaning "when" or "while") and taxat (from
taxere meaning to "assess" or" castigate") meaning "while he
taxes", where the subject is clearly understood to be John
Donne (Dun). In the second line duntaxat is both the adverb
"simply" and the clause "when he (Donne) taxes".   In the
fourth line duntaxat is primarily the adverb but the clause
is still understood, the point in the sense being that when
Donne taxes he has more than one first (because he makes
more than one attack) in English (in Pseudo-Martyr (1610),
Ch. 4) and in Latin in Ignatii Conclaue (1611) to which Cam-
pion alludes in his title.   The sense of the joke may seem
feeble but the skill of the epigram lies in the way in which
the neo-Latinist manipulates Latin syntax to play upon both
meanings of duntaxat in parallel positions at the beginning
of the pentameter line. The 'interlingual' joke was doubt-
less intended as an appropriate compliment to Donne for his

bilingual expertise,   a learned   pleasantry which   could be
expected to appeal to Donne's own   sense of humour.   If this
explanation of the interlingual wit of the epigram is on the
right lines, it is unlikely that any significant distinction
is   intended between   Donne's tone   and purpose   in the   two
works (the Latin is more satirical).   <u>Ridet</u> seems simply to
be a variation upon <u>taxat</u>.   Campion could have written <u>lin-
gua</u> <u>taxat</u> <u>at</u> <u>Ausonia</u>,   but   this would have been repetitious
and cacophonous, altogether too much of a good thing.

Book One

(Notes are keyed to the lines of the Latin text but to the
words of the translation, except for the small number of
textual notes.)

14.   'Solyman'. Campion seems to be referring to the victory over
the Turks at the battle of Lepanto (1571).   It was the one
major victory over the Infidel enemy in the sixteenth cen-
tury and was celebrated by, among others, King James himself
in his poem "The Lepanto" - reprinted in   1603. (See James
Craigie, ed., <u>The</u> <u>Poems</u> <u>of</u> <u>King</u> James <u>VI</u>, Vol. I, Scottish
Text Society, Third Series 22 [Edinburgh, 1955]).   Emrys
Jones comments interestingly on the significance of the vic-
tory and poem in "<u>Othello</u>, <u>Lepanto</u> and the Cyprus Wars", in
<u>Aspects</u> <u>of</u> Othello, ed. Kenneth Muir and Philip Edwards
(Cambridge, 1977).   Unfortunately the Turkish Emperor was
not Solyman the Magnificent, but his successor, Selim II.
Since no-one defeated Solyman, it can only be concluded that
Campion here is making a simple factual mistake.

16ff.'It is his pleasure'.   The near-blasphemous hyperbole can be
paralleled in many other texts.   cf. Joseph Rawlinson, <u>The</u>
<u>Romishe</u> <u>Iudas</u> (1610): "I shall endeauour to fit the treason
of <u>Iudas</u> to the <u>Embryo</u> or <u>incohate</u> treason of this day, next
to it the greatest that ever was" (p. 6).   Francis Herryng,
in <u>Mischeefes</u> <u>Mysterie</u> . . . <u>translated</u> <u>and</u> <u>dilated</u> <u>by</u>
J. <u>Vicars</u> (1617), makes a very similar claim:
      Of blessings <u>spirituall</u>, our blest <u>Saluation</u>
      <u>Wrought</u> by our <u>Sauiour</u>, <u>boughte</u> with's precious bloode,

Was most Diuine, gaue <u>man</u> his cheefest good
Was more admired then the Worlds <u>creation</u>,
But of all <u>Temporall</u> blessings wee enioy'd
Since <u>God</u> did forme the Earth, and <u>Heau'ns</u> high frame,
To our deliverance neuer greater came,
When <u>Rome</u> by <u>Powder</u> would haue vs destroyed.

The cue was given by James himself in his speech to Parliament on November 9: "And now I must craue a little pardon of you since Kings are in the word of GOD it selfe called Gods, as being his Lieutenants and Vice-gerents on earth, and so adorned and furnished with some sparkles of the Diuinitie; to compare some of the workes of GOD the great KING, towards the whole and generall world, to some of his workes towards mee" (<u>The Political Works of James I</u>, ed. C. H. McIlwain [Cambridge, Mass. and Oxford, 1918] p. 281).

30ff. 'The old intractable enemy'. Valesius, in <u>In Serenissimi Regis Iacobi</u> (1606), has a very similar picture of Satan contemplating the peaceful state of Britain:

> Dux Erebi, reprobae parens cui saecula sortis,
> Cum late placidas vrbes, pacataque regna,
> Tranquilla & populos degentes pace videret;
> Quemque sua sub vite, suaeque sub arboris vmbra,
> Auspicijs, IACOBE, tuis, clarissime regum:
> Continuo inuidiae stimulanti incanduit aestu,
> Infernosque furens ad limina tetra ministros,
> Concilium crudele vocat. . . (p. 4)

41ff. 'holy king'. The official title of the Spanish King was "Most Catholic King"; Campion is here obviously being ironic. The 'treachery' which the Spanish King had rejected was the so-called 'Spanish Plot', in which Thomas Winter and Guy Fawkes, together with Tesimond and Owen, were involved at the instigation of Catesby, attempting to solicit the aid of the Spanish government in raising forces to assist a Catholic rising at the death of Elizabeth. Much was made of it in the trial of the conspirators (see <u>Relation</u>, Sig. E2r-3v), though as Albert Loomie makes clear, "before the publication of the Act of Attainder, after the execution of all those accused, few people if any had a full awareness of the 'Spanish Treason'. By then fact was mixed with fiction, false inferences had been imposed on inadequate evidence. When James's muddled version of the entire Spanish affair was made public no one was there to challenge it". See "Guy Fawkes in Spain", <u>Bulletin of the Institute of Historical</u>

<u>Research</u>, Special Supplement 9 (1971) p. 56.

43. 'The Irish'. The crushing of the Irish by Mountjoy had indeed been successful, with the final surrender of Tyrone just after James's accession. Campion's is a cosmetic version of that capitulation.

44. Reference to the 'conspiring arms of the Scots' would seem rather tactless, but it suits the ambiguous attitude to James's uniting of the two kingdoms expressed in Campion's own <u>Lord Hay's Masque</u> (1607).

46. 'the devil soon felt'. Note the similarity of the Devil's anger with that attributed to him in Tasso's <u>Gerusalemme Liberata</u>, Bk. 4:
>   And when he saw their labours well succeed
>   He wept for rage, and threat'ned dire mischance,
>   He chokt his curses, to himself he spake
>   Such noise wild buls, that softly bellow make
Edward Fairefax, trans., <u>Godfrey of Bulloigne</u> (1600) p. 55. See also note to l. 78ff.

76. 'assumes a thousand monstrous shapes'. The linking of the Devil and Proteus is conventional.

78ff.'then growls like a bear'. The picture of maddened Satan draws upon the portrait of the defeated giant, Typhoeus, in Hesiod, <u>Theogony</u>, 830ff: "in all his terrible heads were voices that uttered all manner of cries unspeakable. Sometimes they uttered such sounds as the gods might understand: anon the roar of a bellowing bull . . . sometimes, again, the roaring of a lion of dauntless heart: sometimes noises as of whelps, wondrous to hear: and anon he would hiss, and the high hills echoed to the sound". (Hesiod: <u>the Poems and Fragments</u>, trans. A W Mair [Oxford, 1908] p. 61). Later, Alexander Ross, in <u>Mystagogus Poeticus</u> (1637), asserted simply: "The Devil is the very <u>Typhon</u>" (p. 259).

100. 'This is our invention'. The monkish origin of gunpowder is commented upon by, e.g. John Donne, in <u>Pseudo-Martyr</u> (1610): "as the inuention of Gunpowder is attributed to a contemplative Monke; so these practique Monkes thought it belonged to them to put it in vse and execution" (Sig. B4r). Coke, at the trial, made a similar point: "Gunpowder was the inuention of a Fryar, one of that Romish rable",

Relation (Sig. I4r).   (But in the 1614 edition of Stow's
Annals, [p. 867], Howes comments on the Chinese origin of
gunpowder.)

103. 'two religions'. A standard distinction between the primi-
tive simplicity of Protestantism and the deceptive finery of
Roman Catholicism. See the comparison between Una and Duessa
in Spenser, The Faerie Queene, Bk. I.

109. 'one-eyed'. This depiction seems to fuse the myth of
Echidna, prototype of the deceptively beautiful woman, with
Plutus, the blind god of riches (himself often blended with
Pluto, the god of the Underworld).

114. 'splendid palace'. An echo, perhaps, of Spenser's depiction
of the castle of Lucifera, in The Faerie Queene, Bk. I,
Canto 5.

121. 'barbers'. Barbers' shops were traditionally places of gos-
sip. See Horace, Satires, I.vii.3

122. 'Iphigenia'. The story of Iphigenia was taken by Lucretius,
in De Rerum Natura, I. 85ff., as typifying the way religion
had given birth to unholy deeds. Sandys, in his gloss to
Ovid's telling of the story, in Ovid's Metamorphoses (1640),
reflects: "Superstition is more prevalent than truth in the
blindly devoted. But unadvised vowes are punished in the
performance; not required by God, but perswaded by the
author of impiety" (p. 228).

128. 'But we bear witness'. The model for an age declining into
strife is Ovid, Metamorphoses, I. 145ff. Campion may also
have had in mind Matthew x. 21.

132. 'Triple kingdom'. England and Wales united to Scotland by
James.

139. 'Boniface'. Boniface III, "that ambitious beast" who
"obtained that Rome should be called the Head of all the
Christian Churches", as Vrsinus Joachimus put it in The
Romane Conclave (1609), p. 232. See also Donne, Ignatius his
Conclave, ed. T. S. Healy, S.J. (Oxford, 1969) p.95 and note
p. 106. In his Premonition James sets out to prove that
Boniface III is Antichrist (McIlwain, pp.144-5).

142. 'Heraclitus'. Philosopher of melancholy disposition who weeps over the follies of mankind in contrast to the philosopher Democritus who is said to laugh (see Juvenal X. 34). Campion's version is a variation on the commonplace. The Romish folly is so great that it would either have plunged him into incessant tears or perversely had the reverse effect of making the depressive laugh.

150. 'Catesby'. Campion follows history here, though both Valesius in In Serenissimi Regis Iacobi (1606) and Francis Herryng in Pietas Pontifica despatch their hellish messenger to Fawkes. The centrality of Fawkes as type and epitome of the Plot begins early, as these and other examples show. (See, for example, The Arraignement and execution of the late Traytors (1606), where the last whose execution is gleefully described is "the great Deuill of all, Faulkes alias Iohnson" (Sig. C3v)). But when John Vicars translated Herryng's work in 1617 he added a marginal note: "Fawkes is not heere first mentioned as the Prime Author, but because hee was so inhumane as to be the fatall actor" (Mischeefes Mysterie, p. 5).

152. Grant and Rookwood did not enter the conspiracy until a later stage. See note to line 610.

155. 'notables'. The class-consciousness, which surfaces elsewhere in the text (cf. the description of the mining operation, ll. 416ff), echoes Coke's insistence at the trial that the plotters "were Gentlemen of good houses, of excellent parts, howeuer most pernitiously seduced, abused, corrupted and Iesuited, of very competent fortunes and states" (Relation, Sig. E4v).

161. 'Thamisis'. Normal spelling is Tamesis.

162ff.'Arise'. The address to Catesby is curiously similar to Milton's In Quintum Novembris, 1. 92ff. For both the source may be Mercury's speeches to Aeneas, Aeneid, IV. 267 and 560.

166. 'the laws threaten'. Impending legislation against Catholics was held at the time and since to have been the immediate cause of the Plot. Jenny Wormald, however, points out that: "The Plot cannot have been the consequence of the threat to Catholic laity of a revival of Elizabethan attitudes, for

that is irreconcilable with its known time scale". ("Gunpowder, Treason and Scots", *Journal of British Studies* 24 [1985] p. 152.)

171. 'gods of Ausonia'. "Ausonia" is Italy. The "gods", therefore, are the Catholic saints.

176ff.'he calls together'. Campion fuses the accounts of two meetings of the conspirators as narrated in Winter's confession.

184ff.'We have been acting'. Compare *Relation*: where Catesby "intending to use this so furious and fierie a spirit to a further purpose, doeth as it were stroke him for his great forwardness" (Sig. R2v).

210ff.'Not even if'. An expanded version of Winter's confession, (*Discourse*, Sig. I1r-2v), which does not, however, register any fear at the destruction of Catholics with other victims.

220ff.'Percy rebukes him'. Percy's outburst is taken from Winter's deposition (*Discourse*, Sig. I1v), but the first sentiments, "much blessed . . ." are there given as Catesby's.

229ff.'what could be more just'. This sentiment was alluded to at the trial of the conspirators (*Relation* Sig. H1v), is to be found in Fawkes's deposition (*Discourse*, Sig. H2v), and was picked up by James in his speech to Parliament (McIlwain, p. 282).

241ff.'Proceed with what you are intent'. Sentiments taken from Winter's Confession (*Discourse*, Sig. I2r).

246. 'wise doctor'. Hippocrates.

250. 'if it is acceptable'. In *Discourse* it is Catesby who makes the suggestion of going to meet the Constable (Sig. I1v).

256. 'Owen'. For Hugh Owen, see Albert Loomie, *Spanish Elizabethans* (New York, 1963) Ch. 3. There is little evidence of the intelligencer's direct involvement with the plot, but Loomie cites the Earl of Salisbury's instruction to Coke: "You must remember to lay Owen as foul in this as you can" (p. 89) as indicating the frantic official efforts to taint him with the crime. Coke did his best, asserting that "Owen's finger

hath beene in euery Treason which hath beene of late yeres
detected" (Relation, Sig. E3v.).

274. 'the king's officer will not urge'. A curious sentiment to
     insert here, since the rooms Percy took were in fact used by
     the Commissioners for the Union for meetings in late 1604,
     delaying the beginning of the mining operation.

284. The sacrament administered by John Gerard, who claimed in
     his Autobiography, ed. Philip Caraman (London, 1951) p. 231,
     that he knew nothing of their intentions. His assertion of
     innocence is supported by the testimony of Fawkes and Win-
     ter, though Coke blandly ignored the evidence at the trial
     of the plotters (Relation Sig. H4v).

294. 'humanos'. MS has a full stop after 'humanos'.

306. 'Golden Tagus'. Synechdoche for Spain. The epithet 'Golden',
     standard in classical literature, refers to the golden sand
     of the river.

310. 'Lerna'. Here dwelt the Hydra, a many-headed monster killed
     by Hercules in one of his twelve labours.

310. 'vnquam'. MS reads 'vnguam'.

322. 'teaches the tongue'. For equivocation see Introduction,
     pp. 12-13.

327. 'Pyramid'. A monument erected by Henri IV of France after
     the attempt on his life by Jean Chastel led to the banish-
     ment of the Jesuits, and taken down when they were allowed
     to return in 1604.   In George Hakewill's translation of
     Anti-Coton (1611) we find that the monument was erected
     "before the great gate of the palace, with an inscription
     containing the causes why the Iesuites were banished. In
     which they are termed Heretiques, troublers of the State,
     and corrupters of youth. Which Pyramis while it stood if
     any did aske why it was set up, many more now a dayes are
     ready to aske why it was puld downe" (p. 37). See also Phi-
     lopatris (pseud), An Humble Petition . . . wherein the wan-
     dering ghost of the late Pyramis demolished lately in Paris
     discovereth his hard fortune (1606), in which the ghost of
     the Pyramid asks for lodging and re-erection in England.

332. 'the base hand of one of them'. Alludes to the assassination
     of Henri IV in 1610 by Ravaillac. In much contemporary writ-
     ing the complicity of Jesuits in both the Gunpowder Plot and
     this assassination was asserted, and the link was used to
     intensify the propaganda against them.

340. 'Garnet'. Henry Garnet, born in 1555, returned to England in
     1586, and quickly became Superior of the Jesuits, on the
     arrest of William Weston. Philip Caraman offers a sympa-
     thetic account of his life in Henry Garnet, 1555-1606, and
     the Gunpowder Plot (London, 1964).

341. 'gives judgement etc.'. Alludes to the letters of commenda-
     tion Garnet would write for Catholics travelling abroad.
     The fact that Garnet provided such letters for various of
     the plotters was used as evidence of his complicity in the
     Plot at his trial (Relation, Sig. Z2v, and again in Nor-
     thampton's Speech, Sig. Aa1r-v). His answer was: "And for
     sending of Letters, and commending some persons thereby, he
     confessed he did it often . . . without knowing either
     their purposes or some of their persons: for he neuer knew
     M. Wright for whom he writ" (Relation, Sig. X2r).

342-3 'Belgium submits'. Taken from Relation, Sig. F1r.

349. 'beautiful woman'. Anne Vaux. Suggestions of improper con-
     duct with their female protectresses by Jesuits were common-
     place. Garnet movingly responded to the calumnies of Anne
     Vaux in his speech from the scaffold (Relation, Sig. Fff2v).
     For an account of her life and support of Garnet, see Philip
     Caraman, Henry Garnet, passim.

371. 'does not hesitate to entrust the whole crime'. This was
     precisely the point at issue at Garnet's trial. He insisted
     that Catesby offered to tell him "in particular what attempt
     hee had in hand, if hee would heare it; Which afterwards he
     offered to doe, but Garnet refused to heare him" (Relation,
     Sig. X3r).

376. 'Sicilian Tyrant'. Phalaris. See Ovid, Tristia, III.ii.41ff.

381ff.'author of various double meanings'. Repeats Coke's charge
     that the conspirators "were allowed and taught by the
     Iesuites to equivocate vpon Othe, saluation or otherwise,
     and how then should it be discouered?" (Relation, Sig.

V3r).

406. 'Rejoicing in such great authority'. Responsibility for the
Plot was laid at Garnet's door because of his answer to Cat-
esby. Coke said: "this resolution of Garnet . . . was the
strongest, and onely bond, whereby Catesby afterwards kept
and retained all the Traitors in that so abominable and
detestable a conspiracie" (Relation, Sig. R3v). The Earl of
Salisbury asserted: "what encouraged Catesby that hee might
proceed, but your resoluing him in the first Proposition?
what warranted Fawkes, but Catesbies Explication of Garnet's
arguments?" (Sig. Y3r), and Northampton returned to the
topic later (Sig. Aa3r-v).

414. 'prementis'. MS has 'prementis.' The line continues over the
ruled margin, and the stop seems to indicate only the end of
the line.

419ff.'Fawkes himself'. In rather convoluted fashion Campion
refers to the fact that Fawkes, out of the country since
1593 and hence unknown in London, was entrusted with guard
duty, taking the name John Johnson, and pretending to be
Percy's servant. He persisted for some days after his arrest
in maintaining his alias. Alius rather than alter (which
almost invariably means "one of two") would have been more
usual here.

433. 'maiden princess'. Princess Elizabeth.

435ff.'They raise the spectre of hopes to come'. The discussion
of the hopes of help comes direct from Winter's confession
(Discourse, Sig. I).

441. 'her visit to the tomb of Elizabeth'. Elizabeth's tomb was
not completed until 1606. Her body rested first in the
chapel of her grandfather, Henry VII. Camden in his Reges,
Reginae, Nobiles, et alii (1606 ed.) gives a description of
the tomb and its inscriptions. At the time of the plot,
then, it would seem that the tomb was unfinished, and the
marble effigy not yet in place. Campion's slight anachronism
is, no doubt, consciously entertained.

447ff.'She became most famed'. The summary praise of Elizabeth
reflects the inscription on her tomb: "RELIGIONE AD
PRIMAEVAM SINCERITATEM RESTAVRATA, PACE FVNDATA, MONETA AD

IVSTVM VALOREM REDVCTA, REBELLIONE DOMESTICA VINDICATA,
GALLIA MALIS INTESTINIS PREACIPITI SVBLEVATA, BELGIO
SVSTENATO, HISPANIA CLASSE PROFLIGATA, HIBERNIA PULSIS
HISPANIS ET REBELLIBUS AD DEDITIONEM COACTIS PACATA . . .".

456ff.'restored the rites'. See Campion, Ad Thamesin, ll. 10-11.

473ff. 'Neverthelesss may your bones'.   A very puzzling passage.
I can find no evidence of any actual attempt to desecrate
the remains of Queen Elizabeth. Campion seems to be alluding
metaphorically to the way in which her name was blackened in
Catholic propaganda, typically by Robert Parsons.   In The
Iudgement of a Catholike Englishman (1607), a work aimed at
James's An Apologie for the Oath of Allegiance, he picked up
the King's words:"hauing now sacrificed, as I may say, to
the Manes of my defunct sovereign", and proceeded to demo-
lish the myth of Elizabeth. He contrasted her life with the
lives of true saints and concluded: "If these things were
the ancient wayes to lyfe, and to euerlasting saluation:
then must the pathes of Q. Elizabeth, which are knowne by
most men, to haue byn, eyther wholy different, or most oppo-
site to these, lead to an other opposite end".   He then
works up to a picture of "her lamentable end", a passing to
eternity "with so small sense or feeling of God, in neuer so
much, as to name him, nor to suffer others to bring any
speach thereof . . . is so pittifull an end, as can lightly
fall to a Christian soule". Finally, and this may explain
'the tombe of your father' in the passage, he drags up the
statute made in her father's time "wherein it is declared,
not only by the iudgement of the King, and of all that Par-
liament, but by the iudiciall sentence also of Archbishop
Cranmer, she was pronounced, to be vnlawfully borne, and
that her mother was neuer King Henryes lawfull wyfe" (pp.
27-36). It certainly seems to have been this particular
text which caused considerable anger, and was continually
returned to by Protestant writers. So, for example William
Barlow, in An Answere to A Catholike Englishman (1609) calls
Parsons "A carrionly curre, entring her Tombe, and exenter-
rating her very bowels to stanch his rage: yea, as if he
were the Porter of Hades" (p. 68). William Leigh, in Queene
Elizabeth (1612), speaks of the need to rescue the Queen
from the "blasting breath of the Papists" who think "it is
not sufficient to glut themselues with the blood of their
Soueraignes, vnlesse with their buried bones they might ran-
sacke their blessed soules" (Sig. A4v). John King, in his

Oxford sermon of 1607, dilates on the theme when speaking of Jesuit plots against Elizabeth: "that then they gave her not leaue to liue, now not leaue to be dead, and to sleepe in hir dust, but are angry at hir very manes

Nec mors mihi finet iras

Saeua sed in manes manibus arma dabe

that they haue ript vp from hir cradle, runne through hir life to hir graue, and will needs go down into hell to seeke hir immortall & now immaculate, incorruptible soule amongst hobgoblins and infernall spirits (you know my author)" (p. 33). James himself, the occasion of Parson's diatribe, referred to it in the Premonition added to the reprint of his tract, saying that he will not describe it, as "it abhorres not to raile, nay to rage and spew foorth blasphemies against the late Queene of famous memory" (McIlwain, p. 114). The fact that this dispute postdates the Gunpowder Plot is perhaps not a significant reason for excluding the possibility of Campion's referring to it in this speech, despite the clear anachronism of line 477, 'these recent events'. But there still remains a niggling uncertainty, since the text does seem to suggest an actual, rather than metaphorical attempt upon her tomb.

516. 'sing of you in the churches'. See Hebrews, ii. 12.

522-3.'nor . . . ever incline to sleep'. See Ps. cxxi. 4.

526. 'deferred the appointed council'. In December 1604 the Parliament, originally summoned for February 1605, was prorogued until October.

538. 'beer barrels'. The Latin zithi is a rare word from the Greek, meaning a malt drink, probably the nearest equivalent in the wine-drinking ancient world to beer.

543. 'new suspension'. Campion's timetable is a little shaky here. After the December prorogation the mining and the discovery of the adjacent cellar proceeded. The plotters dispersed in March, and it was not until September that the further prorogation of the Parliament to November was issued. But Fawkes's confession links the March disbanding of the conspirators and the announcement of the prorogation (Discourse, Sig. H3).

566. 'Stanley'. For Sir William Stanley, soldier adventurer, see

Loomie, Spanish Elizabethans, Ch. 5.   He had certainly been
involved with the 'Spanish Treason', but there is little
evidence to connect him with the Powder Plot.   Indeed Winter
in his confession reports that Fawkes met Owen, but did not
see Stanley.

575. 'gives him letters'. See note to 1.341

578. 'an envoy is sent'.   Sir Edward Baynham was sent to the Pope
in August.   Garnet at his trial   claimed that he went "to
informe the   Pope of   the distressed   state of   Catholics in
England" (Relation, Sig. R3r), but at the earlier trial of
the conspirators and at Garnet's trial it was asserted that
Baynham, "an Embassadour fit both for the message and the
person, to be sent betwixt the Pope and the deuill" (Sig.
D1r), carried news of the Gunpowder Plot itself.

583. 'they pray for the swift return'. Alluding to Garnet's much
cited prayer at Coughton on All-Hallows Eve, which included
the hymn Gente auferte perfidam. Garnet claimed that he was
concerned merely about impending anti-Catholic legislation.
James in his speech referred to "certaine formes of prayer
hauing likewise beene set downe and vsed for the good suc-
cesse of that great errand" (McIlwain p. 112). Northampton
accused Garnet at his trial: "you gaue order for a prayer to
be said by Catholikes for their prosperous successe" (Rela-
tion, Sig. Bb1v).

589. 'Fame tells'.   We have not been able to locate a precise
source for this depiction of the two lakes of tears. It may
perhaps have been suggested by the description of the
doubleness of watery effects in Ovid Metamorphoses, XIV.
308ff.

603. 'laethum'. The plant referred to here (whence comes Sardonic
laughter) was usually identified by the ancients as ranuncu-
lus, ("crowfoot"). Laethum, which is not in usual or botan-
ical dictionaries remains a mystery. The Colchian poison is
sweet probably because it is associated with the enchant-
ments and love potions of Medea who came from Colchis.

610. 'entice more'. Campion compresses the timetable of recruit-
ment.   Keyes had joined in November 1604, Robert Winter,
John Grant, and Bates were added at the beginning of 1605,
Christopher Wright in February 1605.   Bates's confession to

Tesimond and the Jesuit's later revelation of the conspiracy to Garnet under the seal of confession provided the key point in the implication of the Jesuit Superior in the Plot. Francis Tresham (who almost certainly betrayed the plot), Sir Everard Digby and Ambrose Rookwood were only enlisted after preparations were complete, in September 1605 - largely because they brought money to the conspiracy, and offered the necessary help for the conduct of affairs in the immediate aftermath of the explosion.

615. 'Tesimond'. Oswald Tesimond (1563-1635) used the names Greenway and Greenwell as aliases. Proclamation was issued for his arrest, but he escaped.

615. 'though wavering'. In Relation, Sig. G3r it is Rookwood who is said to be uncertain.

630. 'while the fates allowed'. Prince Henry died in 1612.

631-2. 'the Duke'. Charles was only 4 years old at the time - the compliment is for later consumption.

643. 'with clothing'. The anonymous figure is described only as 'of a reasonable tall personage' in Discourse, Sig. F1r.

650ff. For the elision of time here, see Introduction, pp. 7-8.

668. 'next morning'. This most flagrant distortion of the time-scale derives directly from Coke's assertion "Now was the letter with the L. Mountegle, whose memorie shall be blessed, on the fourth of November: by the prouidence of the Almightie, not many houres before the treason should haue bene executed, was it fully discovered" (Relation, Sig. S3v).

680. 'lost clothes'. The account in Discourse, Sig. G4v, states: "And yet for the better colour and stay of rumour in case nothing were founde, it was thought meet, that vpon a pre-tence of Whyneards missing some of the Kings stuffe or Hang-ings which he had in keeping, all those roumes should be narrowly ripped for them". The Queen's clothes are not men-tioned in any of the official documents. They do, however, turn up in the version of Francis Herryng's poem, Pietas Pontifica, translated by A.P. as Popish Piety (1610), where "vestes . . . Regales" is rendered "stolne garments of the

Queenes" (p. 81).   This may be   evidence that   Campion con-
sulted this particular poem as a source for his work.

Book Two

16. 'monstrum'. MS reads 'monstrum.'. As in I.   414, this line
    runs over the margin and the stop indicates perhaps only the
    line-end.

31ff.'the tombs   of kings'.   The author   of Discourse   says the
    explosion would have destroyed "not onely our present liuing
    Princes and people, but euen our insensible Monuments reser-
    ued for future ages. So not onely ourselues that are mortal,
    but the immortall Monuments of our ancient Princes and
    Nobilities, that haue bene so preciously preserued from age
    to age, as the remaining Trophees of their eternall glorie,
    and haue so long triumphed ouer enuious time,   should now
    haue beene all consumed together" (Sig. E3v).   Northampton
    too commented on the possible destruction of Westminster
    Abbey, (Relation, Sig. Eee1v), and later writers waxed simi-
    larly indignant. (See, for example, Francis Herryng, Mis-
    cheefes Mysterie, p. 27.)

40ff.'Searching, etc.' The account is closely based on Discourse,
    Sigs. G4v-H1r.

61. 'Suffolk'. The compliment to the Earl of Suffolk, Lord Cham-
    berlain and one of Campion's chief patrons, is an echo of
    Discourse, Sig. G2r. There he is praised for his first
    search of the cellar - an incident which Campion omits.

64ff.'All the treachery'. The speech attempts to capture the
    "confused haste" with which Suffolk is said to speak in
    Relation, Sig. G4v.

67ff.'O glory of kings'. The extravagant praise of James as semi-
    divine is, of course, the staple of panegyric. That Campion
    is relatively restrained may be seen by comparison with this
    extract from George Marcelline's The Triumphs of King James
    (1610): "Heere doe I see my selfe rauished in spirit, and

rapt vp to _Heauen_, the _heauen_ of the most high maiesty of _Great Brittain_, the Epicicle most eleuate of his Royalty. That is to the _Daix_ or State of his _Throne-Royall_, where I see the God of our Worlde ruling all the Motions, the Aspects, the influences, & the Coniunctions of all the starres in his heauen . . ." (pp. 8-9).

80. 'to renew year after year'. James instituted a special liturgy for November the Fifth. One of the prayers reads: "Can this thy goodnesse, O Lord, bee forgotten, worthy to be written in a pillar of Marble, that wee may euer remember to praise thee for the same, as the fact is worthy a lasting monument, that all posteritie may learne to detest it?". But note that 'Philopatris' in _An Humble Petition_ as early as 1606 suggests that "the rituall Monuments of publique prayers religiouslie ordained by his sacred Maiestie to be celebrated through all his Kingdome . . . appeares almost in the verie beginning to bee neglected, both in Court, Countrie, and Citie" (pp. 39-40). Later preachers of November 5th sermons frequently betray a similar anxiety.

87. 'those of small understanding . . . '. In John Stow, _Annals_ (1614 ed.), it is recounted that: "The Council . . . gaue order to the L. Maior of Lon. and the city of Westminster, to set a ciuill watch at their gates: the common people muttered, and imagined many thinges" (p. 878).

90ff.'Digby devises a hunt'. See _Discourse_, Sig. L2r.

103. 'tender years'. Princess Elizabeth was nine years old at the time of the plot.

111ff.Princess Elizabeth married Frederick, Elector Palatine, in 1613. (For the marriage Campion wrote _The Lords' Masque_, which is similarly complimentary to this 'goddess'.)

113. 'mother of sons'. Elizabeth's first son was born January 1614, her second in December 1617. It is, of course possible that Campion's plural _natorum_ represents no more than a pious hope for her future fertility; if, however, it represents factual knowledge, then this is a significant line for the dating of the poem.

115. 'Harington'. Sir John Harington, Lord Harington of Exton, was the guardian of Princess Elizabeth at Combe Abbey. He

accompanied her on her journey with her new husband, and
died at Worms on 23 August, 1613 on his way home to England.

127. 'Ellesmere'. Thomas Egerton, Lord Keeper and Lord Chancel-
lor, created Baron of Ellesmere in 1603. I can find no con-
temporary printed record of his speech. The Journal of Sir
Roger Wilbraham reports Ellesemere's speech. Contrary to the
suggestion of Campion's version, Ellesemere apparently began
with detailed discussion of the business the House had
expected to discuss, the question of the Union of England
and Scotland, and only latterly turned to recent events:
> But what thankfulness in us,   alas Winchester is wit-
> nese of the first attempt of Rawley &c.: & we have
> sene the horrible attempte the last day against king,
> nobles, prelates & commons.
>   This procedes both first & last from romish pristes
> by a hellish practise under the earth.
>   These have raized a nomber like Catelyn's camp of
> wasters & spend goods to stirre rebellion, not so wise
> as Balaam's asse, who discerned God's army: praied the
> king for seuere iustice ne pars sincera trahatur: the
> papistes may be Christians but corrupt romish Chris-
> tians.
>   Millions have geven ther hartes to the king to ayde
> him with ther goods & lands & sacrifice ther lives for
> his service:
>   He praieth exemplarie punishment in these may cause
> others to abhorre romishe religion: & praieth Christ
> Jesus to preserve his maiestie & progenie for ever.

(Camden Miscellany, X [1902] pp.   72-73.)   It may be that
Campion did have access to some record; but it is equally
possible that he attributes to Ellesmere sentiments that
were fairly generally held, and were expressed for example,
by Coke at the trial (Relation, Sig. H1v), more vehemently
in W. Leigh's Great Britaines Great Deliuerance (1606), and
typically by the author of Lucta Jacobi: "Away then (Sir)
with too much of your olde Clemencie, the most dangerous
Companion that euer your Maiesty caried about with you, how-
soever a part desiderated in many princes" (p. 32).   It is
clear, however, that Campion does no violence to the known
attitudes of Ellesemere. A convert from Catholicism, he yet
maintained a consistent anti-Catholic campaign, patronising
many Protestant writers. See Louis A. Knafla, "The 'Coun-
try' Chancellor: The Patronage of Thomas Egerton, Baron
Ellesmere", in French R. Fogle and Louis A. Knafla,

Patronage in Late Renaissance England (Los Angeles, 1983)
pp. 38-54.

168. 'starlike girls'. Alludes to the fact that Princess Mary was
alive at the time of the Plot. (She died in 1607.) Both are
mentioned in Relation, Sig. A4v.

166ff.'And in what darkness'. The contemplation of what would
have happened if the Plot had succeeded is a standard rhe-
torical topos for writers on the event. W. Leigh, in Great
Britaines Great Deliverance (1606), for example, wrote:
"Servants had ruled ouer vs: and none could haue deliuered
us, out of their hands: our inheritance had bene turned to
the strangers, and our house, to the Aliants . . . In our
English Rama, had bene a voice heard mourning and weeping
and great howling . . . We should ere this, haue drunken our
water by measure, and eaten our bread by waight, our skinne
had bene blacke as an Ouen, because of the terrible famine,
they had defiled our women in Sion, and our maides in the
Cities of Iuda" (Sig. B4r).

181ff.'O mildest of Kings'. James prided himself on his mildness,
and his propagandists never tired of reiterating his mercy
towards the Papists. But James himself recognised the
nature, even the justice, of fears such as these when, in An
Apologie for the Oath of Allegiance, he wrote: "my Gouerne-
ment ouer (Papists) since hath so farre exceeded hers, in
Mercie and Clemencie, as not onely Papists themselues grewe
to that height of pride, in confidence of my mildnesse, as
they did directly expect, and assuredly promise to themse-
lues libertie of Conscience, and equalitie with other of my
subiects in all things; but euen a number of the best and
faithfullest of my sayde subiects, were cast in great feare
and amazement of my course and proceedings, euer prognosti-
cating and iustly suspecting that soure fruite to come of
it, which shewed it selfe clearly in the Powder-Treason"
(McIlwain, p. 76).

190ff.'The pious monarch arose'. Campion's version of the King's
speech is curtailed, partly as compliment, but noticeably to
give an altogether fiercer, more anti-Catholic version of
words which, though full of self- congratulation, are nota-
ble for their insistence that all Catholics cannot be tarred
with the same brush as the conspirators.

230. 'tragic straine'. To see the Plot as a 'tragedy' is a com-
      monplace - Coke,   for example, asserted that the Plot was
      "beyond all example whether in fact or fiction, euen of the
      tragique Poets, who did beate their wits to represent the
      most fearfull and horrible murthers" (Relation, Sig. D2v).
      James himself, Northampton and a host of other writers use
      the term. Campion's elaboration is, however, an original
      extension of the image.

231ff. 'Hercules etc.'. In the Hercules Furens of Seneca, Hercules
      puts on the shirt impregnated with deadly poison by the Cen-
      taur Nessus which had been given to him by his wife Deianara
      in the mistaken belief that the poison was a love potion. In
      Seneca's Thyestes Atreus avenged himself upon his brother
      Thyestes, who had seduced his wife, by serving up his sons
      to him for dinner. Both plays, translated by Jasper Heywood,
      had been performed on the Elizabethan stage.   The story of
      Althea is told in Ovid's Metamorphoses, VIII. 445ff. When
      she found that her son Meleager had killed her brothers, she
      threw on the fire a brand (Campion uses Ovid's word stipes)
      which at her son's birth the fates had decreed would be cot-
      erminous with his life. William Gager made this the subject
      of his play Meleager written in 1582, performed in 1592 and
      printed in 1597.

247. 'turgessere'. Normal spelling is 'turgescere'.

248. 'Lambeth'. Catesby's house.

288. 'speciosa'. MS reads 'speciasa'.

300. 'a rider'. Bates.

305ff. 'convened a council'. Campion blends together the account
      of the meeting of Garnet and Tesimond at Coughton on Novem-
      ber 6 with the account of Hall's later remarks to Humphrey
      Littleton (Relation, Sigs. S3v and S4v).   Northampton per-
      haps provided the cue, in remarking to Garnet: "was not
      Greenwell with you . . . when you heard of the discouery of
      the Treason? and did you not there conferre and debate the
      matter together?" (Sig. CC1r).

311ff. 'Oh I am afraid'. These sentiments are attributed by Coke
      to the Jesuits in Relation, Sig. F4v, and again in his
      account of the meeting of Garnet and Tesimond, Sig. S3v.

317. 'Who was it who'. Historians concur in believing it to have
     been Tresham who betrayed the plot. But the conspirators did
     not know, though they suspected him.

328. 'plotting before he was born'. Referred to by James in his
     speech to Parliament, and elaborated, for example, in Lucta
     Jacobi (1607): "Thus begunne he also (as did Iacob) his
     wrastling even in his Rebeccaes bellie; to wit, with that
     old Esau, the roote of those rauenous Ruthuens, grandfather
     to this Italian Edomit the late Earle of Gowrie, who preased
     to diuide his Highnesse in and from his mothers wombe" (Sig.
     B3r). George Marcelline, in The Triumphes of King James the
     First (1610) writes: "So in his very birth likewise, he held
     Esau by the heele, & in his Cradle (in imitation of great
     Hercules) he smothered & strangled great store of Serpents"
     (p.43).

333. 'Hall'. Alias for the Jesuit Edward Oldcorne (1561-1606),
     arrested with Garnet. The accounts at the trials make it
     quite clear that he was not present with Garnet at this time
     but was approached the following day by Tesimond. His senti-
     ments were commented upon by Northampton, in Relation, Sig.
     Cc1v-2r. The overheard conversations between Garnet and Hall
     in prison formed a major part of the evidence against Gar-
     net.

342. 'Gerard'. John Gerard (1564-1637). One of the more flambo-
     yant of the Jesuits. He escaped to the Continent immediately
     after Garnet's execution. He is perhaps the least impli-
     cated of all the Jesuits in the Plot. None of the accounts
     mention him as present at this meeting.

352. 'the ghost of Ignatius'. Drawing on the Senecan ghostly tra-
     dition, beloved of dramatists in the period.

379. 'Terrify the Catholics'. In Relation it is specifically Tes-
     imond who "was resolued to do his best endeauors for the
     raysing of Rebellion, vnder this false pretext and colour,
     that it was concluded that the throats of all the Catho-
     liques in England should be cut" (Sig. S3r).

393ff.'He thunders out the names'. Suggestions of Jesuit involve-
     ment with black magic were part of the commonplace abuse of
     the Order. See, for example, A Discouerie of the most secret
     and subtile practises of the IESVITES (1610), where we are

told that "They act devilish plays to terrify the nouices (and once a very Deuill came among them)" (Sig. B1v-2r).

408. 'Antaeus'. Giant wrestler who was invincible as long as he remained in contact with earth, his mother. Hercules learnt his secret, lifted him up and crushed him in the air.

413ff. 'greatest of the Furies'. Allecto, conventionally allegorised as the warlike Fury, (See Conti, Mythologiae, reproduced, with introduction by Stephen Orgel, New York and London, 1979, pp. 113ff.) Campion here alludes specifically to Virgil, Aeneid, VII. 325ff, where Allecto casts a brand at Turnus.

421. 'Nemesis'. Campion's picture is a variant on the standard depiction, which gives her a spear and a "phial with Ethiops".

436ff. 'houses of strangers'. The conspirators stole horses from Warwick Castle, and armour from Hewell Grange, the house of Lord Windsor.

451. 'people of the midlands'. Campion's Latin term gens Cornauia is glossed by Camden's Brittannia (trans. Philemon Holland, 1637 ed.), where the "Cornavii" are "the Regions which in ancient time the people called Cornabii or Cornavii inhabited" (p.560). They contain the counties of Warwickshire, Worcestershire, Staffordshire, Shropshire and Cheshire.

454. 'Greville'. See the account in Discourse: "Sir Fulke Greuill the elder, Knight, as became one both so ancient in yeares and good reputation, and by his Office being Deputie Lieutentant of Warwickshire, though vnhable in his body, yet by the zeale and true feruancie of his minde, did first apprehend this foresaid Riot to be nothing but the sparkles and sure indices of a following Rebellion" (Sig. L4r). Campion seems to have misread the account, which praises Greville for rightly interpreting local disturbance at the stolen horses as sign of something bigger, as indicating slowness of perception.

491. 'Sabrina'. The River Severn. The conspirators moved from Warwickshire, through Worcestershire, to Holbeche House which is in Staffordshire (and rather nearer to the river Stour than the Severn).

501. 'a single Fury'. This Fury is distinct from the earlier
     Allecto. For this picture Campion perhaps drew upon Cicero,
     Pro Sex. Roscio Amerino, XXIV, 67 (a reference he would have
     found in Conti, p. 115).

521ff. The account of Winter's dream comes from Relation, Sig.
     L1v, though the detail of clanging bells is Campion's addi-
     tion.

529. 'Walsh'. Sir Richard Walsh, Sheriff of Worcestershire. The
     account of his offering a truce, being ignorant of their
     full crimes is taken from Discourse, Sig. M1r.

547 'on their knees'. cf. Discourse, Sig. M2r: "then presently
     (see the wonderfull powers of Gods Iustice vpon guiltie con-
     sciences) did all fall downe vpon their knees, praying GOD
     to pardon them for their bloody enterprise".

554ff. 'Percy falls'. Though Campion kills off the right conspira-
     tors, he fuses the arrest of Thomas Winter, Rookwood and
     Grant at the time with the later arrests of Robert Winter
     and Bates, who had fled before the siege.

LIST OF WORKS CITED

The Arraignement and execution of the late Traytors (1606)

Bald, R. C., John Donne: A Life (Oxford, 1970)

Barlow, William, An Answer to A Catholike Englishman (1609)

Bassett, Bernard, The English Jesuits (London, 1967)

Beal, Peter, ed., Index of Literary Manuscripts, 5 Vols, I, Part One (London and New York, 1980)

Boyce, Benjamin, "News from Hell", PMLA 58 (1943) pp. 402-37

Bradner, Leicester, "References to Chaucer in Campion's Poemata", RES 12 (1936) pp. 322-3

(?)Broughton, Richard, A Iust and Moderate Answer (1606)

Camden, William, Brittannia, trans. Philemon Holland, (1637 ed.)

------ Reges, Reginae, Nobiles, et alii (1606 ed.)

Campion, Thomas, The Works of Thomas Campion, ed. Walter R. Davis, (London, 1969)

------ Campion's Works, ed. Percival Vivian (Oxford, 1909)

Caraman, Philip, Henry Garnet, 1555-1606, and the Gunpowder Plot (London, 1964)

Cecil, Robert, Earl of Salisbury, An Answere to Certaine Scandalous Papers (1606)

Clancy, T. H., Papist Pamphleteers (Chicago, 1964)

Conti (Comes), Natale, Mythologiae, reproduced, with introduction by Stephen Orgel (New York and London, 1979)

A Discouerie of the Most Secret and Subtile Practises of the IESUITES (1610)

A Discourse of the maner of the discouery of this late Intended Treason (1606)

Donne, John, The Complete English Poems, ed. A. J. Smith (Harmondsworth, 1971)

------ Ignatius his Conclave, ed. T. S. Healy, S. J. (Oxford, 1969)

------ Pseudo-Martyr (1610)

Fairefax, Edward, trans., Godfrey of Bulloigne (1600)

Fennor, William, Fennors Descriptions (1616)

Fletcher, Phineas, Locustae, ed. Frederick S. Boas, in Giles and Phineas Fletcher: Poetical Works, 2 vols. (Cambridge, 1908)

Gager, William, Pyramis Quinto Novembris 1605, BL Royal MS 12.A.LIX

Gardiner, S. R., What Gunpowder Plot Was (London, 1897)

Gerard, Father J., What Was the Gunpowder Plot? (London, 1897)

Gerard, John, Autobiography, ed. Philip Caraman (London, 1951)

(?)Hakewill, George, trans., Anti-Coton (1611)

Herryng, Francis, Pietas Pontifica (1606, rev. ed. 1609).

Translated by A. P. as Popish Piety (1610), and again, much dilated, by John Vicars as Mischeefes Mysterie (1617)

Hirst, Derek, Authority and Conflict: England 1603-1658 (London, 1986)

Hurstfield, Joel, "Gunpowder Plot and the Politics of Dissent", in Early Stuart Studies, ed. Howard S Reinmuth Jr. (Minneapolis, 1976)

James I, The Poems of King James VI, ed. James Craigie, Scottish Text Society, Third Series 22 (Edinburgh, 1955)

------ The Political Works of James I, ed. C. H. McIlwain (Cambridge, Mass. and Oxford, 1918)

James, M. R., A Descriptive Catalogue of the Manuscripts in the Library of Sidney Sussex College, Cambridge (Cambridge, 1895)

James, Thomas, The Iesuits Downfall (1612)

Jones, Emrys, "Othello, Lepanto and the Cyprus Wars", in Aspects of Othello, ed. Kenneth Muir and Philip Edwards (Cambridge, 1977)

King, John, A Sermon Preached in Oxford, (1607)

Knafla, Louis A., "The 'Country' Chancellor: The Patronage of Thomas Egerton, Baron Ellesmere", in French R. Fogle and Louis A. Knafla, Patronage in Late Renaissance England (Los Angeles, 1983)

Leigh, William, Great Britaines Great Deliuerance (1606)

------ Queene Elizabeth (1612)

Lindley, David, Thomas Campion (Leiden, 1986)

Loomie, Albert, "Guy Fawkes in Spain", Bulletin of the Institute of Historical Research, Special Supplement 9 (1971)

------ Spanish Elizabethans (New York, 1963)

Lucta Jacobi (1607)

Malloch, A. E., "Father Garnet's Treatise of Equivocation", Recusant History, 15 (1981) pp. 387-395

------ "Equivocation: A Circuit of Reasons", in Familiar Colloquy: Essays presented to Arthur Edward Parker, ed. Patricia Bruckmann (Ottawa, 1978) pp. 132-143

Marcelline, George, The Triumphs of King James (1610)

Milward, Peter, Religious Controversies of the Jacobean Age (London, 1978)

Osborne, Francis, The True Tragicomedy Formerly Acted at Court, eds. John Pitcher and Lois Potter, in The Renaissance Imagination, ed. Stephen Orgel, Vol. 3 (New York and London, 1983)

Parsons, Robert, The Iudgement of a Catholike Englishman (1607)

------ A Treatise Tending to Mitigation (1607)

Peck, Linda Levy, Northampton: Patronage and Policy at the Court of James I (London, 1982)

Philopatris (pseud), An Humble Petition . . . wherein the

wandering ghost of the late Pyramis demolished lately in Paris discovereth his hard fortune (1606)

Rawlinson, Joseph, The Romishe Iudas (1610)

Ross, Alexander, Mystagogus Poeticus (1637)

Sandys, George, Ovid's Metamorphoses Englished (1640 ed.)

Speed, John, History of Great Britaine (1611)

Stow, John, The Annals of England, continued unto 1614 by E. Howes (1615)

A True and Perfect Relation (1606)

Tynely, Robert, Two Learned Sermons (1609)

Valesius, M., In Serenissimi Regis Iacobi (1606)

Vrsinus, Joachimus The Romane Conclave (1609)

Weiner, Carol Z., "The Beleaguered Isle. A Study of Elizabethan and Early Jacobean Anti-Catholicism", Past and Present 51 (1971) pp. 2-34

The Journal of Sir Roger Wilbraham Camden Miscellany, X (1902)

Winwood, Ralph, Memorials of Affairs of State (London, 1725)

Wormald, Jenny, "Gunpowder, Treason and Scots", Journal of British Studies 24 (1985) pp. 141-168

LEEDS TEXTS AND MONOGRAPHS

Leeds Texts and Monographs (new series) is published at intervals, one or more publications a year, on topics related to the study of English language and medieval English literature.